THE SOAY OF OU

'What are we, an insignificant island, that such a blessing should have been conferred upon us.'

A Soay Islander, 1854

LAURANCE REED

The Soay of our Forefathers

Birlinn

This edition published in 2002 by
Birlinn Limited
West Newington House
10 Newington Road
Edinburgh
EH3 9DQ

www.birlinn.co.uk

First published privately in 1986

ISBN 1 84158 229 8

British Library Cataloguing-in-Publication Data
A catalogue record for this book is available
from the British Library

Typeset by Edderston Book Design, Peebles
Printed and bound by Cox & Wyman Ltd, Reading

CONTENTS

ACKNOWLEDGEMENTS

My family owned a house on the Island of Soay for thirty years and it was whilst I was living there in the 1980s that this book was researched and written. I was assisted by many people but I would like to thank in particular: my mother, Mary Reed, who left me the house; John MacLeod of MacLeod for granting me access to his family's papers, and Mrs Gouldesbrough of Register House, who was cataloguing the same; the hydrographer of the Royal Navy in Taunton for allowing the use of material relating to the survey of Loch Scavaig; the Rev. Tom Murchison of Glasgow for making available the Minute Books and Annual Reports of the West Coast Mission, and of the Ladies Highland Association; the Inverness Education Authority for permission to consult the Soay School Log Books; Mr and Mrs Gideon MacRae of Glenbrittle House and Mrs Lorimer of Glenbrittle for help with local information; Dr Alasdair Maclean of Lochboisdale and later of Bernisdale, Mrs Donalda Nicholls of Beaverton, Ontario, and Mr and Mrs Andy McCaskill of Irmo, South Carolina for assistance in tracing the story of the McCaskill family; Bill Leah for encouragement with the book; and Ronald Macdonald, Margaret Campbell and Alexander Campbell, all former inhabitants of the island, for answering many questions.

Laurance Reed
January 2002

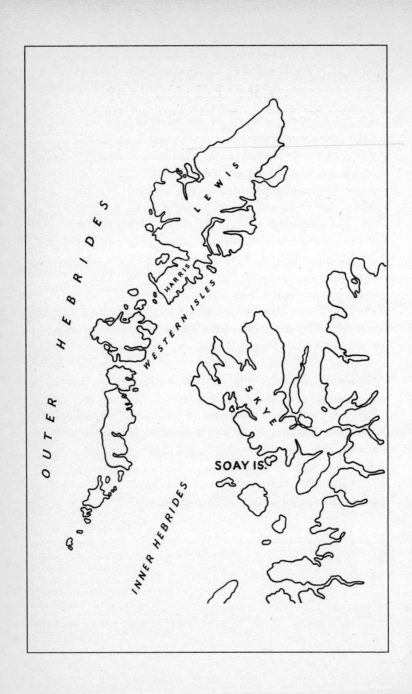

INTRODUCTION

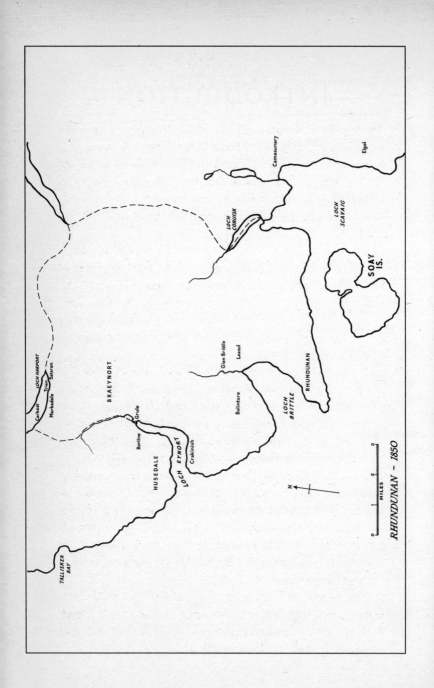

RHUNDUNAN ~ 1850

A BRIEF GUIDE

Among the Hebridean islands of Scotland there are seven small isles which have the name 'Soay'. They are found at St Kilda, Iona, Tiree, Coll, West Loch Tarbert, Loch Inver and the Isle of Skye. The Soay of this book belongs to the parish of Bracadale in Skye. It lies off the south-west coast, directly below the Coolin hills. The map reference is 57°09′ N: 6°13′ W.

The island extends to 2,635 acres and is nearly cut in two by the narrow gash of Soay Harbour. The interior is low and broken, the highest point being less than 500 feet. The coast, by contrast, is bold and rocky, with tall cliffs, deep chasms and caves. The sandstone of these cliffs was quarried in the last century and sent as street pavement to Glasgow and Liverpool.[1]

There are fourteen lochs on Soay and some woodland in the glens and hollows. Birch and rowan are common but there is also oak, aspen and alder. Bluebells, primroses and honeysuckle thrive under the trees. The hills have common ling, bell heather and six species of wild rose. Wet places have flag, orchid, mimulus and five species of willow.[2]

The climate is generally mild – February being the coldest month and May the driest. Rainfall averages about ninety inches a year. The island comes in for its fair share of gales predicted for Malin/Hebrides, especially at the autumnal equinox. The prevailing winds are from the south-west but the locality is subject to violent northerly squalls and sudden changes of sea state.

The waters of Scavaig are rich in sea life. Cod, ling, herring, mackerel, salmon, lobsters and prawns are fished. Seals and otters frequent the shoreline. The killer whale and the basking shark are also present, and the sharks were once hunted from Soay for the oil in their liver. In 1871 a giant sperm whale was stranded on the coast, and in 1950 a beluga or white whale was sighted by two fishermen.

At the top of the loch a short river leads to Coruisk. This famous corry has attracted tourists to Skye since Victorian times. The scenery is written up in all the old guide books. The modern visitor takes a short trip by motor launch from Elgol near Strathaird Point. The pioneers came by row boat from Torrin in neighbouring Loch Slapin – a voyage which took four hours in each direction.

From Elgol the Coolins present a great panorama. The view is often found on calendars and postcards. It is also the label for one well-known whisky. The peaks most easily identified from the island are – the Garsbheinn, Sgurr nan Eag (Peak of Notches) and Sgurr Alasdair (Alexander's Peak). The last, at 3,257 feet, is the highest in the range but there are sixteen peaks above 3,000 feet.

At the foot of the mountains, directly across Soay Sound, is the district of Brittle. There is a single farm there today but at one time there were four townships – Glenbrittle, north of the Greta river; Bolinture (Tower Fold), west of the river Brittle; Leasol or Leisol, where Glenbrittle House now stands; and Rubh' an Dunain (Fortress Point), at the western approaches to Soay Sound.

The first inhabitants at Rubh' an Dunain were neolithic farmers who left a chambered cairn as a memorial to their occupation.[3] They were followed by Iron Age peoples, who built the stone fort which gave the place its name. Norsemen took possession of the Rhu a thousand years later. This part of Bracadale they called Minginish. They also gave Soay its name. It means 'The Sheep Isle'.[4]

Flint arrowheads and burial cists have been found on Soay, showing that it was lived on in the Stone Age. But the island's history starts only in the thirteenth century at the end of the Norse period of rule. At that date it came into the possession of the chiefs of clan MacLeod. They continued as owners for 700 years.

NOTES

1 *Memoirs of the Geological Survey* 'West Central Skye with Soay', 1904.
2 *Proc. of the Univ. of Durham Philosophical Society*, vol. X, 1938–9: and *Trans. of the Botanical Society of Edinburgh,* vol. 36, 1954.
3 *Proc. of the Society of Antiquaries of Scotland,* vols LXVI, LXVIII, 1932, 1934.
4 The famous breed of 'Soay' sheep originate from the isle in the St Kilda group and not from Soay Brittle.

AS OTHERS SAW IT

The scenery in the vicinity of the island has attracted painters and writers. The first of the artists was William Daniell, whose scene of an exploration of Loch Coruisk was exhibited at the Royal Academy of London in 1816. He was followed by J.M.W. Turner, whose watercolour of the same subject can be seen today at the National Gallery in Edinburgh. During his visit Turner lost his footing as he was climbing to get the best view and, by his own account, he was nearly killed. He included himself and his guide in the picture.

Both of these artists came to the district on the advice of Sir Walter Scott, who had visited the area himself while on a yachting tour of the north of Scotland in the summer of 1814. He landed at Camasunary and from there was taken by a farm boy to Coruisk. Scott extolled the scenery as unequalled in any part of the Highlands and he made use of it in his poem 'Lord of the Isles'.

Scott gave fame to the district but he was by no means the first person to record his impressions of the country. As long ago as 1549 Dean Monro wrote a description of the islands in his diocese which included a thumbnail sketch of Soay. Another early account was written by Martin Martin at the end of the seventeenth century:

North eist fra this foirsaid Ile of Rum be twelf mile of sea lyis ane Ile uther half mile lang callit Soabretill, ane roche Ile quhairin deiris uses to be and hunting games, perteining to Mcloyde of Herey. North fra this be twa miles of sea lyis the grate Ile of Sky.[1]

Soa-Bretill lies within a quarter of a mile to the south of the mountain Quillen. It is five miles in circumference and full of bogs, and fitter for pasturage than for cultivation. A mile to the west side it is covered with wood, and the rest consists of heath, grass having a mixture of the mertillo all over. Red garden currants grow in this Isle and are supposed to have been carried thither by birds. There has been no venomous creature ever seen in this little Isle until these two years last, that a black and white big serpent was seen by one of the inhabitants who killed it. They believed it came from the opposite coast of Skie where there are many big serpents.[2]

There is no safe anchorage in Scavaig, this loch, or rather bay, being liable to violent squalls of wind from the Cuillen mountains and the bottom rocky in many parts. There are two small creeks at the head of it where small vessels may lie safe at a hand fast or with one anchor on shore. Each of these creeks is sheltered by a small island but they are of such difficult access that none ought to attempt them without a pilot. With southerly winds vessels may ride near the northeast end of Soa in about 7 to 10 fathoms of water above a cable's length from shore. When the wind is anything northerly very violent gusts of wind come suddenly from the mountains.[3]

Having spent two days examining what was curious in Canna, we sailed for the island of Skye and, after a tedious passage, we landed at Rhundunan, which is about twelve miles from the harbour of Canna. The mountains rise here with the utmost grandeur but the continuous covering of clouds prevented me from investigating them with so much accuracy as I wished. We were glad to take shelter in the first house we came to and luckily we met an obliging man, the shepherd to a gentleman in the army; he lodged us comfortably in his master's almost waste mansion house.[4]

We passed three salt water lochs, or deep embayments and about 11 o'clock opened Scavaig. We were now under the western termination of the high ridge of mountain called Cuillen, Quillin or Coolin, whose weather beaten and serrated peaks we had admired at a distance from Dunvegan. They sank here upon the sea . . . the tops of the ridges, apparently inaccessible to human foot, were rent and split into the most tremendous pinnacles . . . Where we passed within the small Isle of Soa we entered Loch Scavaig under the shoulder of one of these grisly mountains and observed that the opposite side of the loch was of a milder character, the mountains being softened down into steep green declivities.[5]

The Island of Soa contains no attractions of any kind. The anchorage is rendered somewhat grand by the huge masses of the Coolin hills under which it lies. The midges in the Sound of Soa, however, will give full employment in the absence of all other – being the torment of this country, the mosquitoes of the Highlands . . . that their teeth are sharp is too well known, and I can answer for the goodness of their noses. We had anchored about a mile and a half from the shore: yet they scented us, and in about a quarter of an hour, the vessel was covered with this light militia of the lower sky.[6]

Returning on our course we entered Scavaig and cast anchor within the sound of Soa, the greatest Cuillens towering over us though still in clouded majesty. We were on deck by five in the morning and had the satisfaction of finding that although it had rained fiercely all night long, it was now fair, and the mists were rising magnificently from the rocky shore to loftier mountain. The first living object which met our eye was what we at first regarded as a sheep but on taking the glass we found it was a large sea eagle – a very old stager, we doubt not, judging from the whiteness of his head and tail . . . his kingly presence was quite in keeping with the wildness of the surrounding scene.[7]

The dwelling house of Rhundunan, which is situated near the stream which drains the mountain, was nearly destroyed by a debacle which took place in 1855. During a thunderstorm a waterspout broke on three peaks, and soon after a deluge of water was seen rushing over the basin which receives the stream, pouring in one broadsheet of foam down the mountain. To open the doors of the lower part of the house and fly for their lives was all the inmates had time to do before water was upon them to the height of 10 feet – garden, trees and fields near the river were swept away and the place covered with a debris of sand and stone more than a foot deep. Had they not been watching the effect of the heavy black clouds on the hill at the time, and thus got warning sufficient to escape, all in the lower portion of the house must have perished.[8]

The schooner *Woodman* of Berwick on Tweed, Captain Thomas Weatherhead, was wrecked in a very severe gale on the night of Wednesday the 14th instant on the island of Soay, in this neighbourhood. The vessel was laden with slates from Easdale to Leith, and struck upon the east side of Soay where she speedily broke up and now lies a total wreck. The Captain and his wife were both lost, but the crew of two men and a boy came ashore upon part of the wreck. They were very much exhausted and, but for the prompt attention and kindness of the people of Soay, one of them would also have perished. They were carried to houses in the neighbourhood and all their wants carefully attended to. The bodies of the Captain and his wife were found upon the Thursday morning and on Monday conveyed here and decently interred in the burying ground of Kilmorie.[9]

The wife of the manager on the Island kindly received us for the night and gave us a room which they had specially furnished in a cottage beside their own for the accommodation of strangers. In the morning the wind was so strong and the rain came down in such torrents that there seemed little prospect of any one being able to leave the Island that day. But after several hours the weather had so far moderated that we resolved to carry out our purpose. The ferry from Soay to the nearest point of the mainland of Skye is less than two miles and from there to Brittle must be about four. The landing is difficult when there is any sea on the shore as you have to watch the wave and spring from the boat on to the rock. After you have landed the road is really rough but that day it was rougher than usual as the torrents, which come foaming down the side of the mountain here, were greatly swollen. They crossed our path at several points.[10]

The summit of the Garsbheinn is like a knife edge, and so narrow as scarcely to leave room for the erection of a pile. The southeast face forms the arc of a circle to the water's edge, nearly as perfect as could be drawn, with three distinct cliffs separated by steep sloping ledges round which the sheep take their walks but are frequently blown over by the rushing gusts of wind, and killed. During a heavy fall of rain, the south and southwest sides of this hill, which though smooth are exceedingly steep, present a most singular appearance: the dark heavy cloud round its summit is strongly contrasted by a thousand rills and torrents which pour down its sides and form a perfect network, whilst the two swollen burns at its foot, fall over the cliff in broad and roaring waterfalls. Few more awful sights can be witnessed than the view from the anchorage under Soa when during the pauses of a heavy SW gale, the wind and rain suddenly cease, the lower atmosphere clears, and discloses the scene described.[11]

I drove from Portree to Glenbrittle. I tried to get across to the Island but the sea was too rough and the men would not come across from Soay to take me over . . . I walked across the moss of Glenbrittle to the ferry again Saturday morning. I got MacLeod of MacLeod's shepherd to show me the way and we lit a fire to attract the ferryman's attention at Soay. I waited at the ferry from 10.30 until after 2 pm but as there was no sign of a boat coming I returned to Glenbrittle . . . On Saturday the sea was calm, although showery, so there was nothing to prevent the ferry from coming.[12]

1 Donald Monro, *Western Isles of Scotland*, 1549. Herey = Harris. Other early accounts are based on Monro. Thus in 1612 one John Monipenny claimed that Soay was 'profitable for hunting'.

2 Martin Martin, *Description of the Western Isles*, 1703. Red garden currants are not found growing wild today but the island is still free of adders. Mertillo = bog myrtle.

3 Murdoch Mackenzie, *Nautical Description of the West Coast of Great Britain*, 1776. The survey was published in 1776 but actually completed for Scavaig in 1753. Mackenzie employed the ship *Culloden*.

4 Robert Jameson, *Minerology of the Scottish Isles*, 1800. At the time of Jameson's visit Captain Kenneth McCaskill of Rhundunan was serving with the army in Ireland.

5 Walter Scott, *Diary of a Yachting Tour*, 1814. Scott's guide was a farm boy called John Cameron. He was later employed up at Tallisker and died at Husedale by Eynort in 1888.

6 John MacCulloch, *Highlands and Western Islands of Scotland*, 1824. MacCulloch is not precise as to dates but in a lecture he gave in January 1815 he refers to a visit he made to Soay.

7 James Wilson, *Voyage around the Coast of Scotland and the Isles*, 1842. After an absence of several decades sea eagles are again to be seen in the Sound.

8 James Wood, *Remarks on a Survey of Scavaig and Soa Isle*, 1857. In the mid-nineteenth century Glenbrittle House was known as Rhundunan House and is not to be confused with the old McCaskill home at the Rhu.

9 *Inverness Courier*, 22 October 1868. The captain was about forty years old and his wife Helen about twenty-four years. It was a force ten gale and the schooner was seventy tons.

10 John Macphail, *Annual Report of the Ladies Highland Association*, 1872. The sheep manager at this date was Duncan Cameron. MacPhail came to the island to examine the school.

11 *West Coast of Scotland Pilot*, 3rd edition, 1886. This edition was compiled by Lt C.W. Baillie RN but the description is based on Wood's survey of 1857.

12 *Congested District Board Files*, 1901. This official was seeking to get to Soay in connection with the construction of the footpath between the Harbour and the township.

THE HISTORY

CHAPTER ONE

McCASKILL
OF RHUNDUNAN

Sheep have lately been introduced as farm stock and
they promise to do well. They are indeed the only
proper stock for the Cuillen mountain district.

James Macdonald, reporter, 1811

The McCaskills are a family of Norse origin whose common
ancestor came to the British Isles with an invasion fleet a
thousand years ago. He was given a command on the Isle of
Man but, following a violent encounter in that island's
assembly, he was obliged to withdraw and he came to the
Hebrides for safety.[1] In those days Man and the Hebrides
owed ultimate allegiance to the kings of Norway.

In the twelfth century a branch of the family, under the
leadership of Domhnall Dubh, occupied the fortified headland of Rubh' an Dunain in Minginish on Skye. When
Leod, progenitor of the MacLeods, acquired Minginish
through marriage, the McCaskills became his followers.
They were appointed *comes litoris* or wardens of the coast-
line, and in this role they distinguished themselves in the
clan battles of old.

The struggle for territory on Skye between the MacLeods
and the Macdonalds lasted for several centuries. The final
battle was fought in 1601 in the upper reaches of Glenbrittle, just a short distance from the McCaskill stronghold
at the Rhu.

Originally the McCaskills held their land from the MacLeods in exchange for their watch-keeping duties. By the seventeenth century these services had been replaced by rent payable partly in cash and partly in kind. The McCaskills, like other tacksmen, sublet land to lesser tenants but their main source of income came from the raising of native black cattle which were exported to Crieff and other markets in the Lowlands.

Records show that in 1724 seven farms in Minginish were held by individual members of the McCaskill family. Apart from Rubh' an Dunain itself, these farms were – Leasol and Bolinture, both in the Brittle area; Achihard, the whereabouts of which is now forgotten; Braeynort near Loch Eynort; and Carbost and Trien by the shores of Loch Harport.

At about this time it became the practice for all the farms on the MacLeod estate to be let at a given date and for a fixed period of years. When the estate was 'set' in this way in 1754 Rubh' an Dunain and Leasol were united to form a single farm, the whole being called 'Rhundunan'. Further mergers were to follow culminating seventy-five years later in south Minginish being organised as a single sheep farm.

The man responsible for these changes was Kenneth McCaskill, eldest son of John McCaskill of Rhundunan. According to a contemporary account he was 'a rich man and ambitious with it'. He became a JP at an early age and then got involved in politics over the franchise. In 1795 he joined the Royal Fencible Highland Regiment and served with them for five years in Ireland. On returning home he became a captain in the Skye militia. At the age of fifty-six he went to America, where, as he told his lawyer in Edinburgh, he expected to be detained 'for some considerable time'.

On the farm Kenneth continued what his father had begun. At the 'set' of 1792 he obtained an enlargement so as to include Bolinture and part of Glenbrittle. By the end of the eighteenth century Rhundunan farm therefore consisted of Rubh' an Dunain, Leasol, Bolinture, a third of Glenbrittle and the Coolin forest as far north as the Allt Dearg and as far east as Port Sgaile. It also included the island of Soay.

The chief business at Rhundunan remained the rearing of black cattle. Beasts were sold at local fairs and taken south by drovers. The farm had horses and also some native sheep, though no farm on Skye at this date was laid out entirely as sheep pasture. Kelp manufacture was another activity. The best shores were at Soay and Scavaig where the annual yield was estimated to be six tons.

At the beginning of the new century McCaskill began trials with sheep farming. The new breeds were branded with an 'S' and known on Skye as 'Rhundunan sheep'. As early as 1803 Kenneth was complaining to fellow farmers about the cost and delays in getting customs clearance for shipment of wool to Liverpool. A few years later an agricultural expert reported, 'Sheep have lately been introduced as farm stock at Strathaird, Rhundunan, Gesto and Tallisker, and they promise to do well. They are indeed the only proper stock for the Cuillen mountain district. Both the tweedale and the cheviot have been found to thrive.'[2]

This development transformed the prospects for local estates, and at the 'set' of 1810 MacLeod sought a substantial increase in rents. Protests came from every quarter but these were ignored and notices appeared in the newspapers offering extensive farms to let in Minginish: 'A survey and measurement of the land is now making out. Seasoned offers will be received.'[3]

The survey referred to was made by Charles Stewart and covered the whole of Minginish. Rhundunan farm was measured as 442 acres of arable and 26,835 acres of pasture. In the new lease the foxhunter's salary had to be paid by the

farmer, one good farmhouse had to be left at the termination of the let, and kelp rights were to be retained by the
landlord. The rent demanded was £700 a year, the highest
for any farm on the MacLeod estate.

Captain Kenneth accepted these terms for 'Rhundunan,
Glenbrittle and Soay Island as delineated on Mr Stewart's
Plan', but within a fortnight he wrote to MacLeod confess-
ing that he had only signed the new lease in order to give
himself time to look through the world for a spot to rest
upon. Emigration was not to be considered lightly at his
time of life. If the rent could be reduced somewhat he still
hoped to be able to end his days in the glens of Brittle rather
than on the banks of the Ohio.

In the event Kenneth kept the lease and left for America,
taking with him a number of kinsmen and a large party of
his own tenants. He sailed in the autumn of 1811. With war
looming between Britain and the United States, his ship had
to run the blockade of the Atlantic seaboard before reaching
safety at Wilmington, North Carolina.

Years afterwards Kenneth was to be publicly accused of
carrying away his small tenants on a false prospectus and of
selling them off as indentured servants in Charleston.[4] John
Mackenzie, the factor of the estate, was asked what he knew
about this story. He replied:

> I have heard that there were people who left Rhundunan
> many, many years before I was born. They emigrated to
> America. I believe they went of their own accord. It may or
> may not have been the case. I cannot say. The tenant of the
> farm went to America and brought them to his own land
> there, and remained with them 2 years, and then left them, as
> we were given to understand, in good circumstances.[5]

During his sojourn in the United States, Kenneth moved
around a good deal. He stayed in South as well as North
Carolina and at one stage seems to have been resident in the

4

city of New Orleans. In 1821 he returned home to Skye where he negotiated with MacLeod for a renewal of his lease.[6]

It was now decided that Rhundunan should be expanded so as to include the townships of Crakinish, Braeynort, Carbost, Trien and Sataran. The rent agreed was £1,260 a year, commencing Whitsunday 1825. This was calculated on the basis of sales at the recently established Inverness Sheep and Wool Market.

Old Kenneth McCaskill died in 1841, aged eighty-five years. In his will he mentioned property in America, but his assets in Scotland were wholly bound up with the farm. His estate was valued at a little over £5,000, of which sheep accounted for £4,614.

Kenneth was succeeded by his son Donald McCaskill, who had run the farm jointly with his father for the previous ten years. In 1848 Donald emigrated. He went to New Zealand where he joined his youngest brother, Lachlan Allan. The brothers farmed together on land acquired from the Maoris at Hikutaia, south of Thames on North Island. Once he was established, Donald sent for his wife and children.

Donald's successor at Rhundunan was his brother-in-law, Hugh McCaskill. He was brought up on the island of Eigg, where his father was the local doctor. In 1817 Dr McCaskill was drowned in a boating tragedy and shortly thereafter his widow and family moved to Minginish. Hugh took a lease of Tallisker and, enriched by an inheritance from an uncle on Mull, he became one of the leading men in the Skye of his day. He founded the whisky distillery at Carbost and served for a term as factor of the MacLeod estate.

Around 1850 Hugh left Tallisker and went to live at Leasol where his household included two of his sisters, a number of nieces and nephews, one governess, two cooks, one chambermaid, one tablemaid, one pantrymaid, one dairymaid, one gardener and the overseer of the farm. Rhundunan at this date extended to 37,500 acres and employed seventy men.

Four years after his move to Leasol, Hugh surrendered the northern or Glenbrittle division of the farm to Donald C. Cameron. He retained the southern or Rhundunan division in his own hands. After an interval there were further changes in Cameron's favour so that towards the end of his life Hugh was farming a mere 5,500 acres and employing just four shepherds and six labourers.

Hugh died in 1863 and he was the last of the McCaskills to hold the lands of Rhundunan. In the family burial ground at Eynort his headstone records:

> Erected by public subscription to commemorate the important position long held by Hugh McCaskill in the business and social life of Skye, and the respect and affection entertained for him and his wife.

After Hugh's death both divisions of the farm were taken by Donald C. Cameron. The name 'Rhundunan' lingered on for many years but with the link to the McCaskills now gone, the name 'Glenbrittle' came to be preferred as the title of the farm to which Soay Island belonged.

NOTES

1 An alternative tradition has it that these events took place in the Norse settlement at Dublin.
2 J. Macdonald, *General View of the Agriculture of the Hebrides*, 1811.
3 *Inverness Journal* July/August 1810.
4 Evidence to the *Napier Commission*, 18 May 1883.
5 Evidence to the *Commission on Deer Forests*, 21 April 1893.
6 Whilst Kenneth was abroad the farm was managed for him by Ewen Macmillan. His brother, Angus Macmillan, farmed at Camasunary.

CHAPTER TWO

CLEARANCES IN MINGINISH

All the people mentioned in the foregoing
list are really an incumbrance on this
farm . . . I have no use for nor can I get any
remunerating employment for them.

Donald McCaskill, tacksman, 1840

All the early accounts agree that Soay was a place more
suitable for hunting in than for anything else. There would
have been deer and other hunting game but no human
occupants. It is not known when the McCaskills first made
use of it for grazing but Martin Martin mentions some
inhabitants in the year 1695, and it is thought that these
were herdsmen employed by the McCaskills to tend their
stock on the island.

The first head-count was made by the Presbytery of Skye
in 1764. They numbered the inhabitants as just fourteen
souls. Thirty years later, when the *Old Statistical Account* was
compiled, Soay was said to be uninhabited and was described
simply as 'a pendicule of the farm on the shore opposite to
it affording pasture to cattle during part of the summer and
winter seasons'. The account for Bracadale was written in
1792, a year of change on the Rhundunan farm.

In the late eighteenth century the MacLeod estate was in
financial trouble and at the 'set' of 1792 it was decided to
enlarge many of the farms so that they could be let at higher

rents. In preparation for the change decrees of removal were taken out against about 150 tenants in Skye.[1] Among those affected in the district of Minginish were nine joint-tenants at the Glenbrittle township which in that year was joined to Rhundunan. Some of the families were found alternative holdings up at Carbost; others were removed to Soay.

The exact date and circumstances of the occupation are unrecorded but among the first to arrive was a family of Macdonalds. In the year 1876 an aged son, Neil, gave a sworn statement on the matter: 'I am eighty-four years old. I was born at Soay. My father was a tenant at Brittle. When Kenneth McCaskill took the lease the tenants came to Soay.'

The new community established itself rapidly. In the first six years of entries in the *Old Parish Register* (1802–8) the islanders celebrated five marriages. In the same period there were fourteen baptisms within eleven different families. According to the Register, there were four families of Macdonald, three families of Cameron, two families of Maclean, two of Chisholm and two of Mackay, staying on the island at this time. There was also a certain Hector Gillies, who in January 1802 married Ann Martin. Her father, John Martin, was described as a 'tenant in Soay'. In 1792 he had been a tenant of Glenbrittle.

The people were housed in two villages, one at Shepherd's Beach and the other in the Old Village, or Rubha Dubh as it was then known. Between these two colonies there was a solitary house by the Carn burn. The Old Village occupied two acres of waste ground and adjoining it there was a single lot of 'arable moss' extending to seventy-eight acres. At Shepherd's Beach there were ninety acres of 'arable moss' and just over one acre of housing.[2]

Almost all these first occupiers of Soay disappear from the records about 1810, and it is known that some of them joined Kenneth McCaskill's expedition to the Carolinas. There is some indication that the island was vacated for a time but, if so, only a few years passed before it was re-occupied. When the first teacher was appointed in 1817 it was recorded that there were forty-one persons on the school roll, aged between five and forty-five years – twenty-four male and seventeen female.

The first occupants had come from townships immediately across the Sound but the newcomers came from further afield, and mainly from townships on the south shores of Loch Harport. In 1811 these old farms, formerly held by joint-tenants, were split into individual holdings and became the first crofting townships on the MacLeod estate. A condition of the leases was that the tenants would work the kelp shores of Minginish for the landlord. Trouble arose over these clauses and there were threats of eviction.

At Whitsunday 1825 Carbost, Trien and Sataran became part of the Rhundunan farm. MacLeod had bound himself to deliver them free of 'present possessors' and the small tenants involved now applied to the Government for grants of land in Canada and assistance to emigrate. In their petition they stated that they and their fathers had occupied small farms in the parish which the landlord had consolidated as sheep walks. They had no place to remove to and, deprived of land, they were unable to support themselves.

Many years later a correspondent to the *Oban Times* recalled the evictions of this period:

When about 15 years of age, and that is now 60 years since, I accompanied the Sheriff Officer. My duties were to help in filling up each notice to quit and witness each being served upon the tenant. I cannot now remember the number but it must have been considerable when it took us fully three weeks to serve them all. I can well recall that in Minginish it was a wholesale affair . . . doubtless these evictions served still more to increase the poverty existing in already too much congested districts on the sea shore.[3]

At the population census of 1831 the parish of Bracadale contained sixteen tacksmen families and 260 cottar families who 'only possess small patches of potato ground for which they are wholly dependent on the tacksmen'. The number of inhabitants had been climbing steadily for sixty years but in this year a significant fall was recorded. The enumerator, in a footnote to the figures, commented, 'The decrease of the population (334 persons) is attributed to small lots or tenant farms being thrown into large tacks, whereby the inhabitants are obliged to emigrate.'

The first census for which figures are available for Soay is 1841. They show that the population had doubled in twenty years, though most of this had taken place by 1830. There were now 113 people of whom sixty-five were below twenty years of age. The community consisted of thirteen cottars, two agricultural labourers, one boatbuilder, one stone mason, one tailor and five handloom weavers. At least two other families came to Soay in the 1840s, both of them from Sataran. By 1851 the population had reached 158 and this was to be the peak.

Various emigration schemes were mooted at this time. Roderick MacLeod, former minister of Bracadale, was asked for his support. He agreed to give it but in his reply he emphasised that landlords should assist emigrants to Canada and Australia, 'not so much as an act of generosity as of strict justice in which they ought also to be seconded liberally by the tacksmen who now possess the soil upon which the poor people at one time lived in comparative comfort'.

The attitude of the tacksmen to the subject was summed up by McCaskill himself. He drew up a list of the 384 people living on his farm with emigration in mind. At the bottom of the list he added the comment:

All the people included in the foregoing list are really an incumbrance on this farm with the sole exception of those marked 'shepherd' or 'required'. These were put on the list by mistake. I have besides these shepherds and smith, eight other shepherds all with families. As for the other people I have no use for nor can I get any remunerating employment for them.[4]

The 1840s witnessed the great potato famine, and following the widespread destitution this caused the Skye Emigration Society was founded. Meetings were held in every parish to explain to people the advantages of life in the colonies. After one such meeting Hugh McCaskill remarked that on his farm people were lukewarm, and not inclined to move. However one Soay family took advantage of this particular scheme and emigrated to Australia.[5]

It was the middle years of the century which saw the start of organised protest against these clearances. It took the form of a petition to Parliament in which the signatories from Bracadale and Duirinish urged that the attention of the Government 'be directed to the system now too generally pursued of throwing whole districts out of cultivation for game and grazing purposes, and of assigning to the evicted inhabitants small patches of barren land and in many instances no land whatsoever, thus producing idle habits, increase of destitution and periodical famine'.

The petition fell on deaf ears and another thirty years passed before social unrest on Skye forced the Government of the day to appoint the Napier Commission to investigate the grievances of crofters. During 1883 the commission took evidence throughout the Highlands and Islands and in May one such meeting was held at Struan, in Bracadale. The people of Soay sent five delegates and before the meeting they wrote to the Commissioners, declaring, 'No enquiry has ever been made regarding us, and we consider that Providence has sent this Royal Commission to establish the rights of the poor man.'[6]

The commission were given a list of townships in Minginish which had been cleared and they asked for an estimate of the number of people involved. They were told:

There were sixteen families at one time in Crakinish. There were ten or twelve families in Glenbrittle and twenty or more at the Rhu . . . and there would have been six between Merkadale and Trien . . . The people of these townships were scattered through the country and some of them went abroad.

In their report the Napier Commission selected Bracadale as an example of what they called 'consolidation of pastoral areas, accompanied by the removal and dispersion of the humblest class connected with the land'. They were influenced, perhaps, by an anonymous letter posted at Carbost which named twenty townships in the parish that had been cleared during the previous sixty years. The unknown writer declared, 'Plenty of conscience for sheep and no conscience for people. Shame and disgrace when there is plenty of land on Skye.'

NOTES

1 *Scottish Highlander*, 'MacLeod Family Evictions', May, 1893.
2 C. Stewart, *Survey of the Barony of Minginish*, 1810.
3 *Oban Times*, 24 April 1886.
4 There were eighty-seven families in six townships – fourteen at Carbost, eleven at Crakinish, eight at Grule, twelve at Leasol, eighteen at Sataran, and twenty-four at Soay.
5 Roderick MacLeod and family sailed from Liverpool to Adelaide aboard the *Switzerland* in June 1855.
6 The delegates were Alexander McCaskill, John Macrae, John Campbell, and John and Norman Stewart.

CHAPTER THREE

CONDITIONS
OF TENURE

The people are very poor and have wretched
bad houses. They depend chiefly on lobster
fishing. The island is covered with inferior
heathy pasture and is under sheep.

Ordnance Survey, 1877

In the year 1840 Donald McCaskill of Rhundunan divided
his Soay tenants into three groups – five crofters, six cottars
and thirteen landless. He defined a crofter as 'a head of
family who held a lot and paid rent for it', whereas a cottar
'occupied a house, had potato ground and paid rent for it'.
There was little to distinguish the cottars from the landless,
since to keep the latter from starvation, 'I am obliged to give
a quantity of land to each family though I get nothing for
it. Others marked "cottar" are only nominally so as I have
got in all but £5 from them for twenty years' possession.'

The original souming was four milk goats and one cow,
but the tenants also kept sheep and poultry. Later, after a
struggle and threats of eviction, the sheep were taken from
them. The McCaskills, for their part, pastured their sheep
on Soay in the winter months and during the heyday of the
industry, in the mid-nineteenth century, they employed
both shepherds and sheep managers on the island. The
Shepherd's Cot on the north side was constructed to house
the manager.

On the south side the arable ground was divided from the hill by a stone and turf dyke. In the winter it was the practice for the whole of the arable to be thrown open to grazing. The main crops grown were oats and potatoes. All tillage was by the ancient foot plough (caschrom), the land being too rough to turn in any other way.

In 1857 Commander Wood, the Admiralty surveyor, summarised the agricultural position:

> There are a few acres of land round the shores of the bay and on the neck between the two bays where potatoes and a few oats are grown. There is however grass enough on it to support 900 sheep. It is singular that wretched as the soil looks this was nearly the only spot in the Western Highlands which escaped the ravages of the potato disease in 1846.

The people of Soay may have escaped the ravages of the blight, but they did not escape the consequences of it. Widespread destitution was caused by food shortages, and at the height of the crisis every family on Soay was given food aid on a fortnightly basis. Hugh McCaskill of Rhundunan was convenor of the local relief committee and won praise for his work at this time. He gave meal on credit to people and for a large part of this he was never repaid.[1]

The potato famine was an exceptional emergency. Ten years after it was over Commander Wood observed of the general health of the people:

> It is a healthy climate and considering the great amount of moisture and wretched dwellings of the people but little rheumatism prevails; the air is so pure and their habits so simple that when food in sufficient quantity can be procured (and whisky is not too plentiful) I would estimate the general health of the inhabitants as rather above the average.

When Hugh McCaskill died the whole farm went to Donald Cameron, and shortly afterwards it was readvertised in the press as the 'valuable, extensive and well known farm of Rhundunan and Glenbrittle with the Island of Soay, extending to 45,000 acres'. It could be let as one farm or in two divisions. The southern or Rhundunan division was stocked with black-faced and cheviot weddars and the northern or Glenbrittle division with cheviot ewes. 'A great proportion of the grazing is known to be of superior quality,' declared the advertisements.[2]

This was a time of high prosperity for Highland sheep farmers, and Donald Cameron had to pay £1,800 in rent to retain both divisions of the farm. Later he was to lament that he had done very well until he had foolishly gone into competition with speculators and given too big a rent. Then wool went down in price, 'and I have been losing money of late years'.

In Cameron's day there were twenty-one lots on Soay of half an acre a piece. The tenants paid £3 for a lot and the grazing of a cow and £2 for each additional cow. The poverty of these holdings was always a source of complaint and the islanders were at pains to stress this when they went to meet the Napier Commission in May 1883.

John Macrae told the commission that he could put down neither oats nor potatoes on his ground since it was nothing but peats and bogs: 'I tried with carrying some peat on my back to make up soil on my ground but it defied me. I have to pave a way for my cow with stones through my lot in order to get out to the hill.' John and Norman Stewart of the Carri gave their evidence in writing. They stated:

Where we raise our corn has to be manured with seaware just like the potato ground else it would produce nothing . . . It is not possible for a horse to live here so we are forced to carry all the seaware and peats in creels on our backs. No other people on Skye are subject to such labours as we have to undergo.

15

The delegates were supported in their claims by a local minister. Soay, he agreed, was a very poor island and he ascribed the poverty of the tenants primarily to the smallness of the holdings. He was asked if he had observed any solicitude on the part of the landlord or his factor for the welfare of the people. He replied, 'I think they are both very indifferent.'

When Cameron of Glenbrittle gave his evidence he was cross-examined specifically about conditions at Soay. He agreed that hardship sometimes arose when the island became storm-stayed, but he denied that there was any destitution among the inhabitants. On the contrary, 'The people of Soay are supposed to be the best off and the most comfortable in the district from which I come.'

By this date Cameron had held Glenbrittle for thirty years and when the lease expired the next year he did not apply to renew it. From 1884 until 1905 the farm remained in the hands of the MacLeod estate as an unlet subject. The manager was Henry Laidlaw, and in his time the Soay tenants saw some amelioration in their conditions. Rents were reduced by half so that they now paid £1 10s for a 'croft with one cow' and £1 for each additional cow. In 1887 the bill for the seventeen paying tenants came to £33 10s and six families paid no rent. But among the paying tenants there were arrears of £23 10s.

The preceding year the Crofters Holdings Act had become law giving security of tenure to small tenants who held directly of a landlord. The people of the island claimed the benefit of this new Act on the grounds that as the farm was in the hands of the estate they were now tenants of MacLeod and no longer of a tenant farmer. An application was made to the Crofters Commission to fix a fair rent and no objections were lodged. The hearings were held at Struan in Bracadale in 1893.[3]

The commission cut the rents by a third but despite this

concession arrears continued to grow, and at the turn of the century some cattle had to be sold to help clear £83 of unpaid rent. The crofters now sought a further review of their rents. The commission had hoped to visit Soay in 1909 but were prevented from doing so by a violent storm. In the event it was not until 1916 that the Scottish Land Court reviewed the position again.

The homes of the people of Soay were all of the black house type – stone walls without mortar, roofs thatched with heather and held down by ropes. Without fixity of tenure, there was no incentive to improve, and as late as 1877 the Ordnance Survey described the houses as 'wretched bad' and dismissed the Old Village as a 'cluster of huts in very bad repair'. After 1893 however new cottages were built – walls of stone and lime, corrugated roofs, and tongue and groove throughout. The black houses were lit by fish oil burnt in open cruses; the new houses by paraffin lamp.[4]

The grazings were another matter taken up in 1893. The farm manager pastured 500 hoggs on the island in the winter months and the crofters of Soay told the commission that they wanted him to remove the sheep and to leave the island with the people. MacLeod himself was reluctant to give up the grazing rights but indicated that he might be willing to do so if the crofters would take Soay as a complete farm. Discussions on this idea of leasing the whole island to its inhabitants as joint-tenants continued for a number of years but the plan fell through since some were unable to take a share.[5]

In 1905 Glenbrittle farm was let to a new tenant farmer and John Mackenzie, the factor, wrote to the islanders at this time assuring them that by the proceedings of 1893 they had been admitted to all the rights and privileges of the Crofters Holdings Act, and that they would continue to enjoy the fair rent as determined by the commission, and security of tenure, so long as they paid their rents. The position was the same as before except that the farmer was deputed to collect the money.

The new farmer was John MacDonald and as soon as his sheep came to the island the crofters petitioned the Congested District Board for a fence to divide their crofts from the grazings.[6] The factor wrote to the board outlining the position as it then was:

> The crofters of the Island of Soay are subtenants under the farmer in Glenbrittle who has the right of grazing all over the Island. There is no fence separating their crofts from the hill ground on which they also have a right to graze 30 head of cattle. They desire the Board to erect a fence between the arable ground and the hill (about a mile) to keep not only the farmer's sheep but their own cattle from getting at their crops. There was a turf dyke surrounding their crofts but they have allowed it to fall into decay. The men are nearly all sailors and are away for most of the year.

In their own letter to the board the islanders said they wanted a fence to guard their crofts from the sheep and cattle,

> by which last year the most of us had to suffer all our crops to be eaten and destroyed by the sheep, especially the corn . . . there is no use whatever of us trying to plant any crop this year. It is only wasting time and labour. So we look forward in the hopes you will kindly look into this and try to amend our cause.

NOTES

1 At the time of his death Hugh McCaskill was owed £120 by his Soay tenants.
2 *North British Advertiser*, November/December 1868.
3 *The Scottish Highlander*, 'Sittings on Skye', 20 April 1893.
4 The first paraffin lamp was taken to Soay in 1873. John Macdonald bought it from a contractor in Rhum for two shillings.

5 In 1902 Alexander Cameron of Soay made an offer for the whole grazings but no terms could be agreed as MacLeod was uncertain of his ability to stock the land.

6 John MacDonald was a noted breeder of Highland ponies and wrote a book on the subject.

CHAPTER FOUR

FISHING
FOR A LIVING

The inhabitants are good fishermen who
prosecute the long line fishing with more
energy than in other places.

James Wood, surveyor, 1857

Old reports speak of great shoals of herring about the coasts
of Skye, but it seems that local people played only a small
part in exploiting them. In 1792 the minister of Bracadale
stated that very few fish were caught in his area and he
thought this might be due to want of pains or proper
encouragement. A survey made of Skye's western lochs in
1804 found that very little herring was exported in a normal
year but that the inhabitants of these districts consumed
about 1,000 barrels of herring annually.

There were many obstacles in the way of a successful
industry and none more so than the unpredictable behaviour of the herring itself. A report of 1811 noted that the
'arms of the sea of the western shores of Skye were formerly
much frequented by herrings. They have of late been almost
wholly abandoned by that capricious and squeamish fish.'
This was to remain the pattern throughout the century.

The cod and ling at the western end of the Sound pro-
vided a more reliable fishery for the people of Soay. Charles
Stewart, the estate's surveyor, advertised on his map of 1810
'Excellent cod and ling fishing here'. In 1822 a fishcurer

based at Eynort was exploiting these stocks commercially. He had 200 bushels of salt at Rhundunan for the purposes of curing cod, ling and hake fished at the Soay banks by open boats. Five years later he switched his base across to the island with 500 bushels of salt stored in the harbour.

The islanders fished all types of fish for their own consumption, including wrasse which was said to have been their favourite dish. They sold or bartered dried fish with local traders and also gave some to the tacksman in part payment of rent.[1] It is interesting that at the census of 1841 not a single person gave 'fisherman' as their occupation, which suggests that in the early days the people had other employment. But all this was to change as a result of the potato famine. In 1851, fourteen out of twenty-four heads of household gave 'fisherman' as their trade.

During the years of the famine the authorities endeavoured to improve fishing facilities at Soay with a view to making the community more self-reliant. Priority was given to white fish. Under the scheme local crews were loaned twenty-foot boats to enable them to fish distant waters, and fishermen from the east coast came to the district to pass on their skill and knowledge.

The scheme did not go smoothly at all times. In 1849 a letter appeared in the press accusing west coast Highlanders of being slow to profit from it. The correspondent, who was from the east coast, wrote:

> The express object of the mission was to teach the inhabitants the art of fishing successfully so that they may not become a burden to the country. But all attempts by the Board to make them industrious and efficient members of society are rendered utterly futile from their obstinate refusal to become instructed.

The letter brought a rejoinder from a resident of Bracadale who claimed that the very untruth of the statements showed just how anxious people were to find fault with the poor Highlanders. So far from people declining to go with the east coast fishermen, many more had offered their services than they could take. The captain of one of the east coast boats, stationed at Soay, had told her that he could not wish 'for better or more active men'.[2]

During the first season curing was done aboard vessels moored offshore, but the following year a two-level fish store was erected in Soay Harbour, the downstairs for curing and the upstairs 'for accommodating fishermen from any other part of the country that might go to fish from that Island'. The fishcurers themselves came from outside the district. In 1850 Mr Macdonald from Kyleakin cured 140 cwts of cod and ling. In 1851 Mr Mackenzie from Plockton cured 110 cwts.

When James Wood surveyed the island in 1857 he commended the people as 'good fishermen who prosecute the long line fishing with more energy than in other places'. Of the fishing itself Wood remarked:

> The banks between the Island and Rhum afford excellent ground. Cod, ling, skate, hake, conger eels with lobsters and herring in their seasons, can be had in almost any quantity. An attempt is now being made by a company in Glasgow to employ these people in obtaining a regular supply.

The records of the Carron and Skye Fishery District for 1860 show that there were twenty-four fishermen and boys at Soay manning nine boats of an aggregate thirty-two tons. The largest vessel, the *Kitty* of eight tons, had a crew of three. Gear at the station included 45,000 sq. yards of netting – ten nets to a boat, and 9,000 fathoms of line – four lines to a boat. The gear was valued at £216 and the boats at £54. In the harbour the fishermen were supported by a workforce of forty people employed as cutters, packers, carters, net makers and line baiters. At this date Donald McCaskill of Soay was the fishcurer.

In the middle years of the century fishing at Soay had picked up with the reappearance of the herring, but by the late 'sixties this fish had resumed its irregular behaviour. The *Admiralty Pilot* for 1871 observed that the herrings of the Skye coast 'until lately taken in large quantities in the different lochs have now fallen off . . . and recently an important trade for the poor has arisen in the collecting of the common periwinkle'. The men of Soay who stayed at the fishing turned increasingly to shellfish for a livelihood. Others put their knowledge of boats and the sea to good use by serving as seamen on private yachts and tourist steamers.[3]

In 1883 the Napier Commission were given conflicting opinions about the fishing at Soay. Donald Cameron of Glenbrittle insisted that Soay was still a splendid station. When asked if his tenants made much money from it, he replied, 'No, they make just what will keep them alive and that is all they want.' The islanders themselves told Lord Napier that the herring was now gone from local lochs and that they made nothing to speak of at the fishing line. Lobsters were only 'middling' and fetched at best seven shillings a dozen. Whelks were lifted but transport costs to the steamer at Broadford robbed them of much of the profit.[4]

Figures for the last years of the century reveal the uncertain nature of the fishing business. In 1894 the total catch at Soay was worth £567, of which herring accounted for £420, ling £13, eels £1, lobsters £107, and other shellfish £26. Four years later the value of the catch was a mere £202 – almost all lobsters, the herring being very scarce. In 1900 half the value of the catch came from herring but in 1903 the local fishery officer reported, 'Little doing on this Island. The herring fishery was a complete failure and fishermen devoted more of their time than usual to lobster fishing.'

Lobstering had started at Soay in the 1840s and already by 1851 there were four men who classed themselves specifically as 'lobstermen'. In the mid-'sixties the fishery officer for the district found that at Rhum, Eigg and Muck only lobster fishing was prosecuted and that principally by Mull and Soay fishermen. The trade in these early years was necessarily restricted by the problem of getting shellfish to market in a saleable condition. But even in the twentieth century, with improved steamer services, the lobsterman had his problems.

Kenneth McCaskill fished from his two-ton boat the *Rose* and sold his catch to Henry Barber, fishfactor of Billingsgate. His lobsters were taken by mail boat to Oban and thence by rail to London. In 1908 Kenneth received a note with his account informing him that his last box of twenty-eight lobsters had arrived midday Saturday when the market was over. On the box being opened it was found that twenty lobsters were dead but still usable, and three dead and unusable. Barbers paid 1s 3d for a living lobster and 9d for a dead one that was still usable. After deducting 6s 9d for carriage, porterage and commission, Kenneth was left with 14s 6d for his labour.

At the turn of the century there were still twenty full-time fishermen at the Soay station, manning eight boats, with 30,000 sq. yards of net, 13,000 yards of line and 200 creels. The largest boat was the *Sea King* of four tons and the smallest the *Sunrise* of one ton. The schoolmaster was giving lessons in navigation to some of the younger men and on his prompting they wrote to the district office asking if they could have a barometer for use at the station. In his annual report the fishery officer wrote, 'Great care is taken of the instrument furnished gratuitously by the Meteorological Council to the Island of Soay. It is regularly consulted by fishermen engaged in the locality.'

All the fishing boats registered in the Carron and Skye District were sail. The first motorised vessel was registered only in 1908. By the outbreak of the Great War there were twenty. The earning power of the motor vessels was more than three times that of the average sail boat and in his report for 1913 the fishery officer forecast that 'a considerable increase in this type of boat may be looked for'.

Soay took delivery of its first motor-driven fishing boat at the end of the Great War. She was the *Deerpark*, a 24-foot ship's lifeboat fitted with a 5 hp Seal engine with a reversing propellor. She was valued at £150 (as against £5 for the sail boats then at Soay).[5] A second vessel arrived in 1921 and a third in 1922. By 1933 only one of seven vessels at the station was still sail.

There was one further development of note in the inter-war years. In 1930 the landlord leased the salmon rights to Mr Robert Powrie of Perth for £20 a year. This was a bag-net fishery which included the rights on the Skye side of the Sound. Soay was one of a number of stations the Powries had along the west coast. A dwelling house and ice-store were built at the southern end of the township. Operations continued for several decades and gave employment to some islanders.[6]

NOTES

1 There must also have been some curing in the early years for in 1816 Donald Chisholm of Soay was fined five shillings for evasion of salt duty.

2 *Morning Post*, 'Destitution in the Highlands', 29 May 1849.

3 Ten men on Soay in 1871 gave 'seaman' as their occupation.

4 In these years two Soay families had vessels which they used for coastal trading. They were the *Christina* of twenty-three tons (built 1832) and the *Blossom* of fifty-four tons (built 1864).

5 The owner was John Macdonald and on the day of her arrival everyone jumped on board and went for a spin round the island.

6 There was commercial salmon fishing at Soay in the nineteenth century. A legendary 50 pounder was caught and carried in a creel to Brittle for taking away to market.

CHAPTER FIVE

SCHOOLS
AND TEACHERS

Some have gone through all the rules of Grey's
arithmetic though the present teacher has not
been in the Island above two years.

John Shaw, minister, 1822

The Society in Scotland for Propagating Christian Knowledge was founded in 1709 and supported missionaries,
catechists and charity schools in the Highlands and Islands.
In the parish of Bracadale the society was providing at one
time, a teacher, a missionary minister, a catechist and a spin-
ning school. The teacher, Finlay MacEwen, was stationed at
Carbost and in the year 1792 there were forty-two scholars
on the roll. Doubtless a number of persons who later
removed from this district to Soay gained some instruction
at this school.

Early in the nineteenth century several Gaelic school
societies were founded. The Edinburgh society, created in
1811, had as its sole object the teaching of bible reading in
Gaelic. The Inverness Society for the Education of the Poor,
formed in 1818, included writing, arithmetic and English
reading in its syllabus. The schools of both societies were run
on the circulating principle – no teacher remained at one
station above a few years before being sent on to another.

The minister of Bracadale at this time was John Shaw. He
was active in the Gaelic schools movement and reported

GLENBRITTLE HOUSE, HOME OF THE M^CCASKILLS IN THE MID-1800S.

THE CUILLINS, AS SEEN FROM THE NORTH SIDE OF THE ISLAND.

A VIEW OF THE TOWNSHIP AT CAMAS NAN GALL.

SOAY HARBOUR. THE TWO-LEVEL FISH STORE DATES FROM 1849.

THE SCHOOLHOUSE, CONSTRUCTED IN 1878 BY THE BRACADALE SCHOOL BOARD.

THE MISSION HOUSE, BUILT IN 1890 WITH MONEY RAISED BY PUBLIC APPEAL.

THE INHABITANTS OF SOAY PREPARE TO EVACUATE THE ISLAND, 1953.

THE SOAY ISLANDERS ARRIVE AT THEIR NEW HOME, THE ISLE OF MULL, WHERE
THE SCOTTISH OFFICE OFFERED THEM HOUSES, WITH LAND AND FORESTRY JOBS
ATTACHED.

THE POST OFFICE, WHICH OPENED FOR BUSINESS IN JUNE 1891.

A VIEW OF SOAY SOUND FROM THE SUMMIT OF THE BEINN BHREAC.

that in Minginish only 250 people out of a population of 950 had the ability to read. In 1816 he arranged for a teacher of the Edinburgh society to be sent to Brittle. There were twenty-seven scholars on the roll and a number of them came from outlying parts and boarded in the neighbourhood for the advantage of regular attendance. The school lasted for two years but teachers of the society were to return to Brittle on future occasions.

The first teacher at Soay was Norman MacLeod. He came to the island in the summer of 1817 and he too was supported by the Edinburgh society. At the inspection the following year John Shaw reported that there were seventeen boys and thirteen girls in attendance who read extracts from the Old and New Testaments with ease and correctness. Shaw continued:

> As this was the state of the school and as the parents seemed determined to continue the education of their children by providing an English teacher for them, I could not hesitate about the propriety of removing Norman MacLeod. It was with grief they parted with Norman who had been so useful and acceptable to them. They promised they would use their best endeavours to carry on the work which the Society had thus begun.[1]

It was fifteen months later that the islanders secured the services of an English teacher. He was Donald MacQueen, who came to Soay under the patronage of the Inverness society. At the annual meeting of that society in 1822 it was reported that all the inhabitants (save for six aged persons) could by now read and spell Gaelic. Moreover the majority of the boys and girls on the roll had made very good progress in English reading and writing and also in sums. 'Some have gone through all the rules of Grey's arithmetic though the present teacher has not been in the Island above two years.'

MacQueen left Soay soon afterwards but he was to remain in the area as teacher and catechist for a further sixty years. In 1883, at the Napier Enquiry, he was described as a 'hale looking old man who read without spectacles and spoke in a clear and distinct voice'. He died in 1885 aged 100 years and on his tombstone there is an acknowledgement of his early work at Soay.[2]

The Inverness society had its financial problems and a less costly scheme of 'aid schools' was devised under which the society gave a small allowance to parents to help them secure the services of a person qualified to give instruction in the elementary branches. The island was added to the list of such schools in 1831. The teacher was Angus MacNeil and the greater part of his salary of £20 a year was paid for by the islanders. There was by now a school-house – a single storey thatched building with thick stone walls. Attendance averaged twenty-five throughout the year.

Teachers of the Gaelic schools were non-sectarian but at the Disruption of the churches in 1843 trouble arose. Bracadale went over to the Free Church and a Gaelic schools' teacher in the parish was dismissed for no other reason than that he refused to join the ranks of the free secession. The Church of Scotland had their own educational scheme for the Highlands and Islands and in 1845 four of their 'General Assembly Schools' were set up on Skye. One of these was at Soay.

Under the scheme the church paid the teacher's salary but landlords and parents were expected to contribute towards the running costs. Teaching at the Soay School included Geography and Latin and at one point there were as many as forty-three adults and children attending classes. The school continued for six years and for nearly three of those years Samuel Nicholson was teacher.

The General Assembly School of the Church of Scotland was replaced in 1852 by a school of the Ladies Association, a Free Church body founded to aid education in more remote parts of the Highlands. This school lasted, with one short break, until 1878. Continuity at the station was made possible through the generosity of one individual benefactor.[3]

The teachers of the association were all young men training for the ministry. They taught in the summer months and returned to their studies in the winter. Charles Corbet was the first of these students to come to Soay. When the time came for him to return to the university the islanders presented him with twenty-eight pairs of stockings and a barrel of herring for his parents.

A great favourite with the Soay people was Duncan Macgregor. For him they built a comfortable house so that he could pursue his studies quietly by himself in the evenings. Norman MacLeod was the longest serving of the association's teachers. When he went off to college in Edinburgh in 1870 he travelled with a formidable amount of luggage including butter, cheese and herrings for winter use, and more pairs of socks than he could easily wear.

Classes were held in the old Gaelic school building and all the common branches were taught. For several years the school included a sewing department under Mrs McCaskill, wife of the sheep manager. There were thirty girls in her sewing class. Rev. John Fletcher, the Free Church minister, remarked, 'It is exceedingly gratifying to see such a seminary in an Island as remote as Soay where nothing of the kind was ever established before.'

There were annual inspections and the school generally received good and sometimes excellent reports. In 1854 the inspector recorded, 'The correctness and intelligence of their replies bore testimony to Mr Corbet's energy and success as a teacher, and to the diligence of those who enjoyed his services.' In 1871 the examiner said of the scholars, 'the readiness and accuracy of their answers showed a proficiency for which I was altogether unprepared . . . during the absence of the teacher in winter the school is taught by a native of the Island who was educated at the school, and who is now quite capable of conducting it himself'.

The Education Act of 1872 changed the structure of education in Scotland and schooling at Soay now became the responsibility of the Bracadale School Board. The islanders themselves did not take kindly to the change and petitioned the Ladies Association for the return of their teacher. In a carefully worded reply the association pointed out that there was no room for two rival schools on one small island. They expressed much sympathy with the people and added that they were 'very sorry to give up so old and interesting a station'.

The school board began by building a new schoolhouse with classroom and teacher's accommodation under one roof, the site being conveyed by the landlord to the board in a deed containing trusts for education. It cost £606. Running costs of the school were estimated at £70 per annum, of which £50 was the teacher's salary. Parents were expected to make a contribution of a few pennies a week.

The new school started in October 1878 and stayed open for seventy-two years. During this period there were seventeen teachers, six men and eleven women. Miss Elizabeth Simpson was the first of the teachers, and in 1878 there were thirteen children attending her classes. Log Books of the school survive from this date recording daily events – measles, whooping cough, visits, celebrations, convulsions, a fight, a fire, prizes and punishments.[4]

The Education Act made schooling compulsory from five years to thirteen years of age, and in early entries of the log book frequent mention is made of children being kept away from school by their parents to gather whelks, harvest seaware, cut peats, or, in bad weather, just for 'want of shoes'. There was a defaulting officer whose job it was to enforce attendance.

In the late 1880s a row developed between teacher and parents which led to a general boycott of the classes. The parents were taken before the school board but continued refractory notwithstanding. In 1890 two of the parents, Donald Cameron and Donald Macrae, appeared before the sheriff court in Portree for neglecting to educate their children. They told the sheriff that the teaching was so indifferent that they did not think it worth their trouble to keep the children at school. The teacher himself said that a conspiracy had been got up against him.[5]

Language probably had much to do with the troubles at this time. Gaelic remained the language of everyday use on Soay and as late as 1901 a quarter of the population had no other tongue but Gaelic. One of the teachers complained of the difficulty he had in making his scholars understand the substance of his lessons owing to want of English 'of which the most of them can't say a word'. Another teacher insisted that everything had to be translated into Gaelic otherwise all the response he got was 'a stupid-like vacant stare'.

Standards in the class varied from teacher to teacher. In 1879 the inspector reported, 'This school is taught with remarkable care and the results are most satisfactory.' But ten years later the inspector declared:

> The school has not been visited once during the year by any member of the School Board, a circumstance I cannot view otherwise than as disgraceful . . . I do not however say that the negligence of the Board accounts for the unsatisfactory condition of the school for which the laziness of the master must be held responsible in the main.

Donald Kennedy was appointed teacher in 1890 and served at the post for seventeen years. At the start of his term the school was awarded the highest grant for discipline and drill but later, near the end of his stay, criticism was renewed and an explanation sought from the school managers. Steps were taken but morale at the school continued at a low ebb. In 1910 the schoolmaster wrote in the log, 'The parents refuse to send peats and prefer to see the children suffering from cold in a cheerless, fireless room. They don't deserve to have either children, school or schoolmaster.'

With the arrival of Rachel Campbell in 1912 confidence between teacher and parents was restored. On the eve of the Great War the inspector could record, 'A happy change has taken place . . . the children on the roll have been quadrupled in number and the teaching is in bright and intelligent hands.'

NOTES

1 *Edinburgh Gaelic Schools Society*, annual report, 1819.
2 Donald MacQueen was buried in the island cemetery at Snizort.
3 William MacKerrol of Bath gave money to support teaching both at Soay and at Brittle.
4 In November 1940 Donald Maclean was sent home to be treated by his guardians 'for swallowing the brass leg of an alarm clock'. Donald was a wartime refugee from Glasgow.
5 In 1892 Donald Macrae was again before the sheriff for neglecting to educate his sons.

CHAPTER SIX

MISSIONS
AND PREACHERS

Cases of intemperance are scarcely known.
There is not a drop of whisky in the Island.
Pray for this poor out-of-the-way spot.

Lachlan Macrae, catechist, 1870

In the parish of Bracadale there were originally two churches – the kirk of Eynort in Minginish and the chapel of Saint Assint in Bracadale. The church at Eynort was built after the Reformation on the site of an old chapel dedicated to Mael-rubha, an evangelist of the seventh century and patron saint of south-west Skye. The church could seat 200 worshippers and in the year 1792 the district was sufficiently populous for the minister to preach there every second Sunday.

The minister was assisted by a missionary who was stationed at Eynort, and also by a catechist. The missionary preached regularly at the station conducting his services in English and Gaelic in the summer months, and in Gaelic only during the winter. The duties of the catechist were to catechise the young, read with and instruct the old, and visit the sick and afflicted.

In 1823 Roderick MacLeod was appointed minister of Bracadale in succession to John Shaw. Early on he clashed with the presbytery of Skye and was suspended for a time on account of his unorthodox views. But among the poor he won a devoted following and at the Disruption of 1843 the congregation followed his example and joined the Free Church. Roderick MacLeod said of his flock in Bracadale, 'The people in general are shrewd and sagacious, and manifest a good degree of intellect as to the ordinary affairs of life; as to morality and religion it is yet a day of small things.'[1]

A Royal Commission of 1835 found that the missionary at Eynort, Mr Macdonald, preached from time to time at three other places in Minginish, including the island of Soay, but noted that the inhabitants of the area were so situated with regard to the parish minister that they were necessarily deprived of pastoral superintendence.[2] On another occasion the minister himself wrote:

> Stormy seas and rugged mountains exclude the Soay people from all Sabbath privileges, except when I occasionally visit them which from the distance and inaccessible position of the Island cannot be more frequently than once every three or four months.

In the absence of a regular preacher it was left to the school teachers to give religious guidance to the islanders. In 1818 John Shaw had written to the Gaelic Schools Society of Edinburgh commenting:

> It will be gratifying for you to learn that the scriptures are now read in every house on this small island and that family worship, which was altogether unknown there, is now attempted by some of these poor people.

Likewise, in reporting to the Inverness Society in 1822 Shaw wrote:

> The school seems to have produced a considerable reformation in the habits of the people. They meet together for hearing the word of God on the Sabbath, which formerly they did not, and swearing and other bad habits have disappeared.[3]

The student ministers of the Ladies Association school made it their practice to hold two and sometimes three services on the Sabbath, together with a meeting for prayers and exhortation on Wednesdays. Charles Corbet noted that his services were regularly attended by everyone on the island and that the girls looked forward to the yearly distribution of clothes, since this enabled them to go to church properly dressed.

Each year prizes were given at the school for scriptural knowledge. One examining minister stated that in this subject the more advanced scholars were thoroughly conversant: 'They quote book, chapter and verse with perfect readiness in proof of any doctrine, principle or duty bearing on the Christian religion.'

In the 1860s there was something of a religious awakening on Soay, especially among the young. Murdoch McCaskill, the teacher, was the leader of this revival. Later on in life he was to rise to a position of some influence in church affairs.[4] Two boys born on the island in these years were themselves to enter the Church. John McCaskill, son of the sheep manager, was born at the Shepherd's Cot in 1857. John Stewart, son of a crofter, was born in one of the houses at the Carri in 1859. McCaskill became minister at North Ballachulish and Stewart, after a tour of duty in Canada, came home to serve at Tiree, the Small Isles and Skye.

Among missionary societies at work in the West Highlands in these days was the West Coast Mission, founded to promote the spiritual welfare of sailors and fishermen. The early work of the mission was concentrated in the south west of the country. Later, following a journey in the yacht *Friend of the Isles*, the directors decided to extend the work to places with a seafaring population further north. In 1864 Lachlan Macrae of Soay was appointed full-time catechist for the mission. He was paid £10 a year and was required to put in eighteen hours' missionary work each week either at Soay or in Brittle.

Shortly after taking up the post Macrae wrote to the mission in Glasgow, 'I hold two meetings on the Sabbath and one during the week. I visit from house to house, read the scriptures and pray, giving special attention to the sick and the aged who are numerous.' In another year he wrote:

I am glad to tell you that my sabbath meetings are well attended. I find great reverence for religion and their knowledge is increasing. Cases of intemperance are scarcely known; there is not a drop of whisky in the Island. Pray for this poor out-of-the-way spot.

The old school house at Soay also served as a church. In 1871 Rev. John Macphail found that the classroom was fitted up with both pulpit and pews which had been

The furnishing of some ruinous chapel in a district from which the people had been cleared away. The men of Soay thought that they could put the timber to better account and on one of their fishing expeditions they carried the whole of it away with them and put it into the school. For such lawlessness terrible things were at first to be done to them. But when the matter was more calmly considered they were allowed to pass unpunished.

Alexander McCaskill of Soay was to give the Napier Commission his own version of this story.

There was this old church which was destroyed. We took a piece of the old pulpit and one or two pews. The landlord belonged to the Established Church and sent us to Portree. I went there, lost two days, and was sent to Edinburgh, and the authorities there were so kind to us that we were not out of lodgings until we came home.[5]

McCaskill also told Lord Napier that the island had been neglected in matters of religion but this was refuted by a local minister who told the commission that apart from a resident catechist, it was seldom that the island was without

36

the services of a missionary. Indeed it frequently had the services of a licentiate of the Free Church to which kirk all the people of the island belonged.

McCaskill, however, was unrepentant and wrote to the commission after the hearings. He protested:

> I cannot pass over Mr Maclean's boldness in trying to contradict my statement regarding ministerial visitations. He said there is a catechist whereas there is none, only an ignorant colporteur. He also said a missionary. I never saw a missionary on this Island for more than five or six months in a year with the exception of one I would not go to hear myself. He was for two years on the Island doing his master work.

In 1889 the Highlands and Islands Committee of the Free Church sent a delegation to Soay to investigate the position. In their report they strongly recommended that a mission house be built to house a permanent agent. The delegation was told that a respectable contractor had offered to erect a house adjoining the meeting hall for the sum of £87 18s. The report continued:

> If this sum could be raised and the house built it would be an unspeakable advantage to this Island. Donald Murray, our missionary at Uig in Lewis, is willing to take up work at Soay and he would be, in the judgement of all who know him, an admirable man for the place.

A fund raising campaign was duly started. The landlord gifted the land and the islanders themselves gave free labour and undertook to keep the new buildings in repair. The work was finished in time for Donald Murray and his family to take up residence in the spring of 1890. Part of his salary of £40 a year was raised locally by friends of Soay.

The island lost the services of its full-time missionary in 1901, and ten years later the minister of the Free Church, appealing for another resident agent, quoted the ferryman as saying that unless they got a missionary soon, the people would be in danger of forgetting the Sabbath. As a result of this appeal the West Coast Mission resumed their work on the island. The arrangement stood until the 1930s when the Free Church once more appointed their missionaries to serve at Soay.

During the Great War the mission house or manse was occupied and largely rebuilt by a shooting tenant. After his departure it again became the lodgings for visiting missionaries. The meeting hall next door continued to be used for services and weddings but the annual communion of the Free Church was not celebrated on the island; for this the islanders travelled to Struan, sacrament week usually falling in July. There was also no cemetery on Soay. The dead were conveyed by sea to the ancient burial ground at Eynort.

NOTES

1 Roderick MacLeod was translated to Snizort in 1839 and later became moderator of the Free Church.
2 *Royal Commission for Religious Instruction*, 1835.
3 *Inverness Courier*, 'Report of the Inverness Society for the Education of the Poor', 9 May 1822.
4 As minister of Dingwall he led Highland opinion on certain doctrinal questions in dispute at the end of the century.
5 The men of Soay were in fact lodged in the Calton Jail for a spell before being released on payment of a fine.

CHAPTER SEVEN

LINKS WITH
THE MAINLAND

To say that steamers cannot call owing to
navigational difficulties is so much bunkum as
we who have been born and bred to the sea
would never allow it.

Neil Macrae, fisherman, 1937

The people of Soay caught their own fish, grew their own
potatoes and produced their own butter, cheese and eggs.
But other needs had to be imported. The old supply route
was by cart from Broadford to Torrin at the head of Loch
Slapin and thence by boat to the island. Many a time
supplies urgently needed at home had to be left beneath an
upturned boat while the crew waited for the weather to
moderate.

Communication with Soay was not only irregular but
also at times hazardous. In October 1868 the schooner
Woodman was wrecked off the coast during a force ten gale.
The captain and his wife were both drowned. The crew of
two men and a boy came ashore on part of the wreckage,
but one of them was also thought to be dead. However, 'a
young islander wrapped him in his own warm clothes and
carried him to the nearest house where, after several hours
of laborious exertions to restore animation, he recovered'.

The schooner was carrying a cargo of slates and from
time to time wrecks in the area supplemented normal
supplies. In 1899 RMS *Labrador* was wrecked near the

Skerryvore Light. In March the Soay school was closed for a week since so many of the children had gone searching for the wreckage. On another occasion the *Harmony* from Quebec was abandoned and then wrecked in the Inner Hebrides. Her valuable cargo of oak logs and deal was washed ashore in Minginish.

There was also an overland route to Soay. A path ran across the lower slopes of the Coolins from Leac in the Sound to the farmhouse in Brittle. In 1857 Commander Wood wrote:

> Soay Island forms part of this farm but communication with it is neither easy or pleasant and in winter is interrupted for weeks together. Leac affords the only spot in the Sound where boats that communicate with Soay can land . . . that they can do so appears strange as the head of the cove is a collection of great boulders and rough rocks which would destroy the boats of any but such rough and ready customers as these.

The traveller lit a fire to attract attention and sometimes an answering signal was sent from the village to show that a boat was crossing the Sound for him. It is said that at one time each family on the island had their own special knoll on the hillside for kindling fires so that those at home had some idea who was wanting to be ferried across. Similar rules applied for those wishing to get to the island from Elgol.[1]

The land route, too, had its dangers. In September 1872, Jane Chisholm and her teenage son were returning home in the company of a local pedlar. The Allt na Droit burn between Glenbrittle and Leac was greatly swollen by heavy rains. The pedlar succeeded in crossing with difficulty but mother and son were both swept away and drowned. Mrs Chisholm had been carrying part of the teacher's salary. This was missing when her body was found and suspicions were aroused. The report of the procurator fiscal concluded that she had died from drowning and her son from head injuries when carried away by the force of the water. The local minister wrote at the time that the incident had cast 'a sudden gloom over the district and caused much painful feeling'.[2]

Mail for the island came by a variety of routes. The original postal address was 'Soay, by Broadford', but in 1881 John McCallum began running his new steamer *Hebridean* to some more isolated parts of the west coast and included a call at Soay. A new route was thus opened for mail and supplies from the south. By the end of the century weekly calls were being made, and in 1900 the official address was changed to 'Soay, by Oban'.

In 1890 the islanders had petitioned for a post office of their own. This was opened for business on 3 June the following year. The postmaster was Donald Cameron. Deliveries (after 1898) were made by the *Hebrides* every Wednesday at 6 a.m. Outgoing mail had to be in by midday Tuesday ready for bagging. At this date the Soay post office handled all normal services except telegraphic.[3]

The year before the opening of the post office a delegation had gone to Broadford to lobby members of the Highland and Islands Commission who were on a fact finding tour in the area. They asked for a pier and more regular steamer services for the collection of their fish. The commission proposed several changes to the steamer schedules which would have helped Soay but these were not taken up. Accordingly, the islanders wrote to their Member of Parliament with further proposals, only to have them rejected by the Post Office as impracticable.

When the Mallaig railway was opened in 1901 the islanders returned to the subject and the Member of Parliament visited Soay to review matters for himself. As a result of his intervention the Post Office agreed to look again at the case for more frequent services if a steamer run was established at Mallaig for the outlying islands.

Six years later the Member of Parliament received yet further representations. He was reminded that the *Hebrides* called weekly in the course of trading and carried mail and lobster boxes to Dunvegan, where they were transferred to MacBrayne's steamer for transmission to Oban and Billingsgate. He was told that through stress of weather the consignment sometimes missed the connection at Dunvegan. The islanders therefore asked that the mail steamer itself should call at Soay once a week en route to Oban, 'thus providing cheaper transport and removing the cause of so much uncertainty'.

This proposal had the backing of the landlord and also of officials involved in the negotiation. But the plan was scuppered by MacBraynes, who insisted that they could not sail safely round Soay in the dark of winter unless lights were placed on the island to guide their steamers past danger points.

During the Great War there was a general disruption of services and at one time Soay was getting mail and supplies from naval patrol boats based at Mallaig. After the war the islanders renewed their campaign to be included on the main mail steamer run. They failed in this but got instead a supply boat of their own. The *Marys*, skippered by Sandy Campbell, was employed to provide a weekly mail run to Mallaig. The postal address was changed to 'Isle of Soay, by Mallaig'.

In the 1930s the Tuesday supply boat was supported in the summer months by tourist steamers which called twice weekly at Scavaig, and the motor vessel *Soay* was used to ferry cargo and passengers between these steamers and shore. In the winter months the *Dunara Castle* from the Clyde called roughly every ten days, but her trips were frequently interrupted by bad weather and in 1937, after a prolonged rough spell, the islanders renewed their demands to be included on the main mail steamer route.

MacBraynes re-stated their objections of thirty years before – their steamers could not call in the dark as the 'Island cannot be seen at night under the Coolin Hills'. Neil Macrae of Soay retorted that this was 'so much bunkum as we who have been born and bred to the sea would never allow it. There is not another harbour on the west coast easier to negotiate.' The Post Office itself thought that the weekly run by the *Marys* was adequate so far as mail was concerned but they did offer to provide a twice-weekly delivery from Elgol. This was rejected since there was no jetty there.

The *Marys* herself came to an untimely end. In October 1946 she was returning home with the weekly supply of provisions when,

> shortly after leaving harbour flames were seen on board and a rescue party set out to investigate. On the way they met the crew and passengers returning to port in their dinghy. A few minutes later there was an explosion and the burning vessel disappeared. The occupants, who had an alarming experience, were fortunate in getting to their dinghy. The cargo was a total loss.[4]

In the matter of a telegraphic service the Member of Parliament had more success. In 1936 he wrote to the Post Office asking if they could not connect Soay with the telegraph in Glenbrittle by means of an undersea cable.

> It is dreadful to think that people should be living on such an Island and that should a case of illness or accident occur during stormy weather, which abounds in these waters, it should be impossible for a doctor to get to the Island in time to relieve a patient.

The Post Office were sympathetic but demurred on grounds of cost. But the Secretary of State agreed that there was a need for some form of telegraphic communication with the island. Mrs Flora MacLeod, the landlord, lobbied officials at the Scottish Office. After her call one official wrote to another:

> By the way, Mrs MacLeod said that she heard that Soay originally got a Post Office by attracting the attention of Mr Gladstone when he was in the vicinity. Perhaps this is the origin of their belief in the potency of periodical agitation.

In the end a radio link with Elgol was agreed upon, the annual running costs being shared between the Post Office, the Department of Agriculture, the Department of Health, the Skye District Council, and Flora MacLeod. The link was opened on 3 December 1937, and the islanders sent the first message to their Member of Parliament: 'The inhabitants of Soay greet you by radio link to express their appreciation of your efforts on their behalf . . . this is just what was needed to bring Soay into line with more favoured places.'

NOTES

1 Strangers to Soay usually stayed at the whitewashed Shepherd's Cot., where James Wood said, 'a decent bed and a kind welcome can be procured by people benighted on the Island'.
2 The stream was thereafter known as *Jane's Burn*, and the Soay people placed a flagstone across it for the benefit of travellers.
3 Mr and Mrs Kenneth Cameron succeeded Donald Cameron as postmasters. The island had its own post-mark but not its own stamps.
4 *Oban Times,* 26 October 1946.

CHAPTER EIGHT

FAREWELL
TO AN ISLAND

Nobody likes evacuations but the economic
facts of Soay had to be faced. However much
money we poured into the Island we could not
have given the people permanent work.

Lord Home, statesman, 1953

Shortly before the Great War the Island of Soay was let to a
shooting tenant – William Meikle from Edinburgh. He paid
£50 a year for the shootings and £35 for the island. In those
days there was grouse and blackcock on the hill but Meikle
also reared pheasant and partridges. He resided in the
Mission House, which he rebuilt, and kept a yacht in the
Harbour. This was the first time that Soay had been let
independently of Glenbrittle farm.

At the end of the Great War the MacLeods sold off large
parts of Minginish to the Government who wanted land for
the resettlement of ex-servicemen. The estate retained the
Coolin Hills, Glenbrittle and Soay itself. The farm, now
greatly reduced in size, was let first to the Wisharts and then
to the MacRaes. In 1930 the island ceased to be part of the
farm and the grazings were let thereafter to individual
tenants.[1] There was some discussion at this stage about
further sales of land to the Government but there was
apparently no thought about selling the island to anyone.

In 1936 there occurred an event which might be said to

mark the beginning of the end for the people of Soay. The fishing season the previous summer had been a very bad one for lobstermen, and this caused some hardship to those families who depended almost entirely on shellfish for a living. The position was made worse by stormy weather and delays in keeping the island supplied. In December1936 the *Dunara Castle* arrived to find the population laid low with influenza and very short of rations. The captain considered the situation so serious that he radioed for medical help.

The story got into the newspapers. It was claimed that the failure of the summer's fishing, combined with severe winter conditions in successive years, had reduced the people of Soay to a condition 'verging on semi-starvation'. Mrs MacLeod, the landlord, suggested that the reports were exaggerated and in this she was supported by an islander who protested against the claims that there was destitution or extreme poverty on Soay. He said, 'I am honestly ashamed that any such communication should have been sent out.'[2]

As a consequence of all the publicity several people came forward with offers to buy the island. A businessman from Glasgow proposed to make Soay self-supporting by organising the community as a 'cooperative', whilst a retired civil servant from England wanted to bring economic independence and 'culture' to the islanders by investing his entire capital in the place. Mrs MacLeod rejected these offers, but when, some years later, Major Gavin Maxwell wanted to buy the island she agreed to sell. The MacLeods had been landlords since the thirteenth century.

In 1945 Maxwell paid £900 for the ownership of Soay. He had a plan to use it as a base for a shark fishing enterprise. His quarry was the basking shark or sail fish which frequents west coast waters in the warm summer months, and which is valuable for the oil in its liver. The Island of Soay Shark Fisheries Ltd was founded, and a factory built in the harbour to process the oil and other products.[3]

There was nothing new about shark fishing in the Hebrides. Two hundred years ago the inhabitants of the islands were reported to be 'very alert in the pursuit of, and dextrous in killing them'. Their success was attributed to 'the laudable exertions of the Commissioners for Fisheries in Scotland in awarding premiums to boats that extract the greatest quantity of oil'.

But in 1945 no such inducements were on offer and the Soay shark fishing venture was killed off by a fall in the price of oil. In 1948 Maxwell resigned from the business he had created and the company ceased operations the following year. Until 1951 the island was administered as part of the Hamilton and Kinneil estates.[4] In that year it was sold again.

It was in January 1952 that the islanders petitioned the Government in favour of evacuation. A few weeks later a team of officials arrived to investigate and report. The Highlands and Islands Advisory Panel were consulted and agreed to support the petition if arrangements could be made to re-establish the nine families as a 'community' elsewhere in the Highlands. In May an announcement was made to the press.

The chairman of the advisory panel told reporters that it was their policy to encourage people to live in remote out-of-the-way places and to keep the islands populated, but

It is not our view that people should continue to live in places which do not have the economic resources to support them, or which are incapable of redevelopment or rehabilitation to provide these resources. This is the situation at Soay which was never inhabited until the time of the clearances.

The evacuation was organised by the Department of Agriculture under powers given in the Congested District (Scotland) Act 1897. They purchased thirty acres of arable land and 170 acres of rough grazing for the Soay crofters at Craignure in the Isle of Mull. This was by the sea with opportunities for lobster fishing. It was also hoped that the Forestry Commission could provide some jobs. There were twenty-seven evacuees altogether, the oldest being seventy-eight years and the youngest a babe in arms.

During the final weeks the land court came across to assess compensation due to the outgoing crofters. The Free Church minister came to conduct the last of the services. Engineers from the Post Office arrived to close the radio link with Elgol, and the press sailed in boatloads to cover the departure. The last mailbag contained a message from Gavin Maxwell and requests from collectors wanting envelopes stamped with Soay's closing post-date. There was also a telegram from the Member of Parliament in which he said, 'I send you my heartfelt understanding . . . perhaps you may draw consolation from the knowledge that your experience will serve to call nationwide attention to the economic plight of the Highlands.'

The SS *Hebrides* was used in the evacuation. 'All day,' wrote one reporter, 'the Soay islanders have been packing and a quarter of a mile off this stony beach lies the steamer, her slim red funnel fuming as if impatient to be gone.' She sailed after midnight with Soay still visible against the sky of a midsummer night and a piper playing a lament on the deck. The date was 20 June 1953.

All the crofting tenants on Soay had signed the petition in favour of evacuating the island.[5] Inevitably there had been second thoughts and some islanders had made a last minute attempt to get the whole thing called off. But the Department of Agriculture were determined to see it through for as one newsman observed, 'Over the years they had been bombarded by complaints and petitions as if by the shells of an off-lying battle cruiser.'

Nor was the 1952 petition the first call to evacuate. In

1947, after the supply boat *Marys* had been lost, the demand was for better links with Mallaig or transfer as a community to the mainland. Answering a question in Parliament about a new mail boat for Soay, the minister replied, 'The islanders will no doubt consider whether they wish to pursue the suggestion of evacuation in the light of such arrangements as may be found practicable.'

Resettlement had also been on people's minds in 1937. On that occasion the islanders had written to their Member of Parliament urging him to press the matter of a new steamer service before the bad weather came:

> We sincerely trust that you will be able to get this boon granted to us, otherwise we are not prepared to face another winter on the Island. The miseries and hardships of the last are too fresh in our memory. There is only one of two things to be done, either another mail steamer or else take us off the Island and settle us somewhere in the Empire where we will get a chance of living decently.

Even as early as 1883 the Napier Commission had been told that there was a consensus in favour of resettlement. Alexander McCaskill of Soay was asked what should be done if the land was so bad. He answered, 'Remove the inhabitants out of the Island altogether.' The commission asked again, 'Then we distinctly understand from you that you want to be removed?' McCaskill replied, 'We want to be removed.'

When the people of Soay reached Mull they were greeted by Lord Home, then a minister at the Scottish Office. Soay was the first evacuation since St Kilda and the event had aroused fears for the future of other Hebridean islands. Replying to questions from the press Lord Home said, 'Nobody likes evacuations but the economic facts of Soay had to be faced. However much money we poured into the Island we could not have given the people permanent work.'

To this *The Times* of London added the plea that the movement away from the Hebrides should not be complacently accepted for the 'inhabitants of the Highlands and Islands have shown a tenacity in preserving their communities which ought not to be allowed to end in total defeat'.[6]

Most of the people who went to the Isle of Mull stayed there, and held together as a community. So it is fitting that one of them should have the final word. A month after the removal Sandy Campbell wrote to the *Oban Times* to thank publicly all those people who had helped them in their transfer to Mull where, as he put it, 'We hope to find the good fortune which circumstances denied us in our own Island of Soay . . . None of us will ever forget this very momentous occasion of our lives.'

NOTES

1 The first was Neil MacInnes from Strathaird. He paid £30 a year.
2 *Scots Magazine*, 'Survey of Conditions on Soay', December 1937.
3 Shark steaks from Soay were sold by a Glasgow fishmonger at 6d a pound. Other samples went to zoos and dog houses.
4 Maxwell wrote a book about shark fishing and the Hamiltons were partners in the business.
5 The new owners, Mr and Mrs J. Geddes, did not leave at the evacuation but continued to live on the island, first as landlords and later as crofters.
6 *The Times*, 'Retreat from Soay', 30 May 1953.

POSTSCRIPT

In 1951 Mrs Jeanne Geddes bought the island from the defunct Island of Soay Shark Fisheries Ltd and went to live on Soay with her husband 'Tex' Geddes and their young son, Duncan. When the evacuation took place the resident crofters renounced their holdings and Mrs Geddes became liable to pay compensation for their permanent improvements. This was beyond her means at the time and her estate became bankrupt.

The trustee in sequestration disposed of a number of houses on Soay to raise money but in the end the island itself had to be sold to clear the debts. In 1963 the new owner, Dr Michael Gilbertson, agreed to create for Mr Geddes a single farm made up of all but one of the old crofts on the southern part of the island. The new unit was called South Soay and was approved by the Crofters' Commission.

Twenty years later, when crofters became entitled to buy their holdings, Tex Geddes was able to buy back the greater part of what the family had lost through bankruptcy. Dr Nicholas Martin, who purchased Soay from Dr Gilbertson in 1981, completed the sale of land to Mr Geddes after protracted Land Court hearings.

Mr Geddes died in 1998 and the current owner of the South Soay croft is Duncan Geddes. He left the island some years ago and went to live in the Orkneys, where his wife Diane had been born. Since his departure the population has declined and today only one family is resident all the year round.

Oliver and Donita Davies and their two sons reside on the north side of the island at the head of Strangers' Bay. Oliver has lived on Soay for nearly forty years and fishes from his boat, the *Golden Isles*, landing his catch thrice weekly at Elgol. Donita hails from the Orkneys and before her marriage was the island's school teacher. The family own their croft and are entitled to buy from Dr Martin their share of the common grazings.

MAIN SOURCES

CHAPTER ONE

Book of Dunvegan by R. MacLeod, 1939.
Clan MacLeod Magazine, 'The MacAskills of Rubh' an Dunain', vol. 2, 1951.
Commissary Court Records.
MacLeod Muniments, Rentals and Leases.
Register of Deeds.
The MacAskill Family by A. & D. MacCaskill, 1984.

CHAPTER TWO

Decennial Census for the Parish of Bracadale.
MacLeod Muniments, Rentals, Leases and Emigration.
Napier Commission, Report and Evidence.
Old Parish Register for Bracadale, 1802–1854.
Survey of the Barony of Minginish by Charles Stewart, 1810.

CHAPTER THREE

Congested District Board Files, 1902–1906.
Crofters' Commission, Annual Report, 1893.
MacLeod Muniments, Rentals and Leases.
Napier Commission, Report and Evidence.
Remarks on a Survey of Scavaig and Soa Isle by James Wood, 1857.
Scottish Land Court, Abstract of Proceedings, 1916.

CHAPTER FOUR

Board for the Relief of Destitution, Reports, 1848–1851.
Board of Fisheries for Scotland, Annual Reports.
Carron and Skye Fishery District Records.
Remarks on a Survey of Scavaig and Soa Isle by James Wood, 1857.
Merchantile Navy Lists.

CHAPTER FIVE

Edinburgh Gaelic Schools Society, Annual Report, 1819.
Ladies Highland Association, Minutes and Annual Reports, 1854–1878.
Inverness Society for the Education of the Poor, Annual Reports.
Scottish Education Department Records.
Soay School Log Books, 1878–1950.

CHAPTER SIX

Bracadale Kirk Sessions, Minutes.
Highland and Islands Committee of the Free Church, Reports, 1881–1901.
Ladies Highland Association, Minutes and Annual Reports, 1854–1878.
Royal Commission on Religious Instruction, Report and Returns, 1835.
West Coast Mission, Minutes and Annual Reports, 1864–1930.

CHAPTER SEVEN

Board of Agriculture Files.
Congested District Board Files.
Glasgow Herald, 26 October 1937.
Inverness Courier, 22 October 1868, 3 October 1872.
Ministry of Transport Records.
Skye's Postal History by J. Mackay, 1978.

CHAPTER EIGHT

Harpoon at a Venture by G. Maxwell, 1952.
Glasgow Herald, 10 February 1936, 30 December 1936, 19 January 1937, 2 February 1937, 26 October 1937.
Oban Times, 24 May 1952, 27 June 1953, 18 July 1953.
Picture Post, 21 September 1946, 11 July 1953.
Scotsman, 19 June 1953, 20 June 1953, 22 June 1953.
Scots Magazine, December 1937, June 1953.

APPENDIX

NOTES ON THE McCASKILLS

The first McCaskills to emigrate to America were a party of brothers who, with their families, voyaged to the New World five years before the American Revolution. They settled in North Carolina and by the time of the 1784 census there were McCaskills residing in four counties in that state – Anson, Richmond, Montgomery and Moore. Around the year 1800 several of these families resettled in Kershaw and Chesterfield counties in South Carolina.

The head of the family when these emigrations began was John McCaskill of Rhundunan, who died on 23 February 1775. He was married to Catherine MacLeod, who died on 10 December 1796. John was succeeded by his eldest son Kenneth who was to hold the farm for more than sixty years.

Kenneth was often styled 'Captain Kenneth' in recognition of the years he spent with the British Army in Ireland. Later he emigrated to America, taking a large number of tenants with him. His ship, the *Chalmette* or the *Charlamaine*, reached Wilmington, North Carolina in November 1811.

On arrival some of the immigrants went directly to South Carolina where they joined kinsmen living in Kershaw county. Other families remained in the northern state. At the beginning of the war of 1812 they were registered as British aliens living in Moore, Richmond and Robeson counties.

During his sojourn in the United States Kenneth moved around a good deal. One of his sons was born in the city of New Orleans and another son was born in South Carolina. In 1821 the family returned home to Scotland.

Kenneth was married to Christina MacLeod of Leasol.

She died on 9 October 1838, aged fifty-five years. McCaskill himself passed away on 1 March 1841, aged eighty-five years. They were buried in the old churchyard at Eynort.

In his will, made before his wife's death, Kenneth divided his estate into five shares. He gave one share to his spouse 'Christina MacLeod or McCaskill'; two shares to Donald, 'my eldest lawful son'; one to Jane, 'my only daughter'; and one to Lachlan Allan, 'my youngest son'. Three other sons, Kenneth, Alexander and William, all in Upper Canada 'have already received from me a fair and just share of my means and estate, and have been authorised to realise my property in America'.

Kenneth, Alexander and William had emigrated to Canada in 1830. They built the first mill in what today is the village of Cannington, Ontario. In 1840 they moved on to Beaverton by Lake Simcoe, where they were joined from Scotland by their sister, Jane.

In 1879 a local paper published the following details about the family:

Died at the residence of her brother, Mr William McCaskill, on November 7th last, Miss Jane McCaskill in the 72nd year of her age. She was born at Rhundunan on the Isle of Skye, Scotland. Her father was a Captain in the British Army. Two of her brothers are stock raisers in New Zealand; another brother was, when last heard of, engaged in the China and Australian Works. Her uncle by the father's side was a Major-General and for sometime a Governor in the West Indies. The McCaskills were in possession of Rhundunan for a long line of generations. A lease of this place is, or lately was, in the possession of the family dating as far back as the 12th century.

According to Canadian records Jane's brother William was born in New Orleans in 1813, and died at Beaverton on 10 November 1883. He was survived by his wife Flora and six daughters. The *Woodville Advocate* commented:

Mr William McCaskill, one of the pioneer settlers of Thorah, was laid to rest on Monday last. Coming here when the township was in its infancy, he was one of those who boldly faced the hardships of the times and hewed for himself a home from the forest which then spread over the entire township, and of those through whose exertions the township has attained the prominent position it has.

When old Kenneth died the farm in Scotland passed to Donald McCaskill. On 17 January 1838 he married his second cousin, Colina McCaskill, who was the youngest daughter of Dr Donald McCaskill of Arisaig and the Small Isles. When the census was taken three years later Donald and Colina were living at Leasol with two small children.

In 1848 Donald entrusted his wife and young family to the care of his brother-in-law, Hugh McCaskill, and sailed to New Zealand, where he joined his youngest brother, Lachlan Allan. The brothers farmed together at Hikutaia which lies fifteen miles south of Thames on North Island.

In April 1855, Colina and three of the children, Christina, Kenneth and Jane, set out for London to take ship to New Zealand. Two other sons, Hugh and Donald, stayed on Skye with their uncle Hugh and only went out to join the rest of the family after his death. A sixth child, John Malcolm, was born in Auckland in 1857.

Donald senior died on 24 February 1883. The *Thames Star* noted his passing:

> Our obituary column today contains a notice of the death of one of the oldest settlers in the district, Mr Donald McCaskill of Hikutaia, who died at the ripe age of 75 years. Mr McCaskill was a native of the Isle of Skye and arrived in these parts some thirty years ago. He acquired from the natives a piece of land at Hikutaia on which he and his brother Mr L.A. McCaskill have resided ever since.

Lachlan Allan died on 17 August 1887, aged seventy-one

years. His death certificate reveals that he was born in South Carolina and that he had been in New Zealand for forty-eight years. Colina died in her eighty-first year. She was buried in the Shortland Cemetery at Thames on 30 September 1897.

In the 1880s the four sons of Donald and Colina were living at Hikutaia where they were engaged as farmers and bushmen. The youngest son, John Malcolm, died in April 1904 and was buried at Thames. Donald junior died at Paeroa on 25 May 1914 and was buried there. On 8 May 1916 Hugh died at Paeroa and was also buried there. Kenneth, the eldest son, expired on 29 July 1918 and was buried at Kauri.

LANDLORDS OF SOAY, 1772–1951

1772–1801	General Norman MacLeod
1801–1835	John Norman MacLeod
1835–1895	Norman MacLeod
1895–1929	Norman Magnus MacLeod
1929–1935	Sir Reginald MacLeod
1935–1945	Dame Flora MacLeod
1945–1947	Major Gavin Maxwell
1947–1951	Island of Soay Shark Fisheries Ltd

FARMERS OF GLENBRITTLE, 1775–1929

1775–1841	Kenneth McCaskill
1841–1846	Donald McCaskill
1846–1863	Hugh McCaskill
1863–1884	Donald Cameron
1884–1905	MacLeod of MacLeod
1905–1921	John MacDonald
1921–1929	Frederick Wishart

NOTE: The Island of Soay formed part of Glenbrittle farm throughout this period, except between 1911–1917 when it was leased separately to William Meikle. In 1930 it ceased to belong to the farm.

SOA ISLAND

Surveyed by Charles Stewart for John Norman MacLeod, 1810.

Lot		*Acres*
185.	Murish Pasture	667.1
186.	Pasture	6.8
187.	Arable, moss interspersed with spots of pasture	89.5
188.	Mossy Pasture	6.9
189.	Mossy Pasture	18.5
190.	Mossy Pasture	8.0
	Houses	1.2
191.	Arable, moss interspersed with spots of pasture	78.2
192.	Murish Pasture	1480.1
	Houses and waste ground about them.	2.1
	TOTAL	2358.4
	Arable	167.7
	Pasture	2187.4
	Housing	3.3

NOTE: the original survey is in the MacLeod Muniments but a copy is held by Register House in Edinburgh.

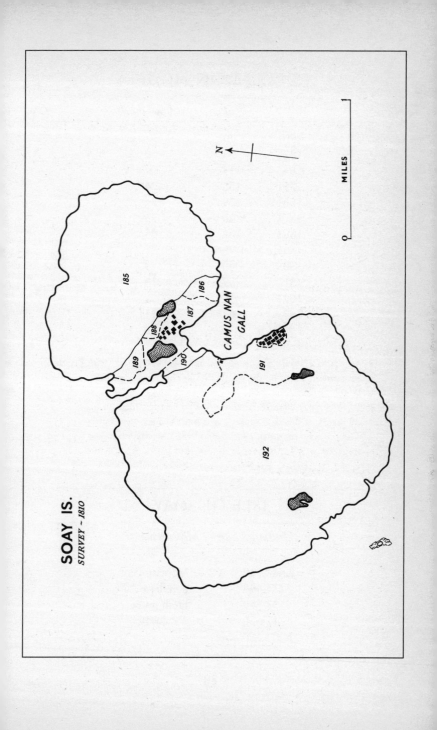

SOAY IS.
SURVEY ~ 1810

185
186
187
188
189
190
191
192

CAMUS NAN GALL

N

0   MILES   1

POPULATION FIGURES

Year	People	Households
1801	70[1]	12
1821	50[2]	9
1841	113	22
1851	158	24[3]
1861	129	24
1871	120	26
1881	102	25
1891	78[4]	21
1901	60	19
1911	57	13
1921	51	12
1931	64[5]	11
1951	30	10

1 An estimate based on baptisms and marriages in the Old Parish Register.
2 An estimate based on the number of families at Soay in 1821, as given by the teacher.
3 In 1854 there were 28 families – the highest recorded number.
4 29 people at this date spoke Gaelic only; the rest were bilingual.
5 There was no census in 1941 but in 1937 the population was reported to be 76.

ISLE OF SOAY

Ordnance Survey Measurements

2,464.940	Moorland etc.
124.490	Foreshore
32.580	Fresh water
12.650	Tidal water
2,634.660 *acres*	

FISHING BOATS
STATIONED AT SOAY, 1895

Boat	Owner	Tonnage	Length
Sea King	Angus Macdonald	4 tons	24 feet
White Heather	Alexander Cameron	4 tons	24 feet
Jessie Campbell	John Campbell	2 tons	18 feet
E. Macrae	Angus Cameron	2 tons	17½ feet
Rose	Kenneth McCaskill	2 tons	16 feet
Star	John Macdonald	1½ tons	16 feet
Wild Duck	John Stewart	1½ tons	16 feet
Sunrise	Donald Macrae	1 ton	16 feet

NOTE: 8 boats employed 20 fishermen, 30,000 yards of net, 13,000 yards of line and 200 creels. Boats and gear valued at £183.

TOWNSHIPS AND FARMSTEADS
WITHIN THE BOUNDS OF THE
RHUNDUNAN/GLENBRITTLE FARM

Buabisgil
Salacharie
Sataran
Trien and Mercadal
Buaile Shuainn
Carbost
Carbost Bheag
Buaile na Clach
Gortan an Fhirich

Brae Eynort
Gruille
Brunnal
Crakinish
Gleann Breatal
Rubh' an Dunain
Leisol
Achadh a' Bhaird
Buaile an Tuir

SCHOOL TEACHERS

Gaelic Schools Societies

Norman MacLeod (1817–1818)
Donald MacQueen (1820–1822)
Angus MacNeil (1831–1835)

Church of Scotland General
Assembly School

George Morrison (1845–1846)
Farquhar Mackinnon (1846–1848)
Samuel Nicholson (1848–1851)

Free Church Ladies
Highland Association
School

Charles Corbet (1852–1854)
John Stewart (1854–1855)
Donald Mackenzie (1856–1858)
Murdoch McCaskill (1861–1862)
John Monro (1862–1865)
Duncan Macgregor (1865–1867)
Nicol Nicolson (1867–1869)
Norman MacLeod (1870–1875)
Donald Mackay (1876–1878)

Soay Public School

Elizabeth Simpson (1878–1880)
Maggie Taylors (1880–1882)
John MacLeod (1883–1885)
James Christie (1885–1887)
James Campbell (1887–1890)
Donald Kennedy (1890–1906)
Catherine Kennedy (1906–1908)
James Mackinnon (1908–1909)
Norman Matheson (1910–1912)
Rachel Campbell (1912–1919)
Margaret Morrison (1919–1924)
Rebecca Maclean (1924–1926)
Margaret Ferguson (1926–1929)
Clementina Macdonald (1930–1936)
Marion Campbell (1936–1939)
Alexandrina Macdonald (1939–1944)
Margaret Campbell (1944–1950)

CHURCH MISSIONARIES

Free Church

West Coast Mission

John Nicholson (1879–1881)
Donald Murray (1890–1899)
Farquhar Mackenzie (1899–1901)
Calum Murray (1932–1934)
Neil Macdonald (1935–1939)
Donald Mackay (1939–1942)
Donald Macrae (1942–1945)
Robert Kennedy (1945–1948)
Norman Matheson (1948–1951)

Lachlan Macrae (1864–1890)
Angus Mackinnon (1912)
John Macdonald (1913–1914)
John Ross (1915)
John Macdonald (1916–1919)
Malcolm Morrison (1920–1922)
Murdo MacLeod (1923)
Malcolm MacCaulay (1924)
Kenneth Maclean (1925–1930)

SOAY TENANTS 1840

With comments supplied by the tacksman.

Neil Campbell – cotter, 'This is a useful man being a carpenter and boatbuilder yet is an incumbrance having paid but £5 for 20 years: and that pittance only by work: is a fit subject for emigration.'

John Chisholm – cotter, 'This is a very useless person though young and healthy, but I think him honest.'

Alexander Cameron – no land, 'An excellent person with promising family: but very poor.'

Donald Maclean – no land, 'A good workman but has nothing to do.'

Donald Morrison – no land, 'A very poor but able man, precisely situated as above and consequently begging for the whole summer.'

Roderick Campbell – no land, 'A miserably poor man: is a widower.'

Harry Chisholm – no land, 'This family is sickly and consists of an old woman, two poor girls – piteable objects – and their two brothers.'

John Stewart – no land, 'A half-witted man and an imbecile sister.'

Donald Macdonald – no land, 'A person of industrious habits: but I have no wish to prevent him getting another situation.'

All the above are really a burden on me.

John Cameron – no land, 'A sickly man though young and has a poor asthmatic brother living with him'.

Ronald Macdonald – cotter, 'Is an unmarried man supporting an aged mother: his sister is an honest lass.'

Neil Macdonald – cotter, 'This is an honest man and I wish him well elsewhere.'

Christopher Mackay – crofter, 'A stout able man but unfortunately has acquired a bad name, and can never leave home but at the risk of his neck.'

Alexander Campbell – crofter, 'A rascal though of good parents, is young and able.'

Roderick MacLeod – cotter, 'A very good and obliging young man.'

Catherine Campbell – no land, 'An old maid'.

Norman Morrison – cotter, 'An obliging young man but has paid £1 in rent for his holding in ten years.'

John Mackay – crofter, 'A poor old man and wife with an excellent son.'

Widow Mackay – no land, 'A very poor person though young.'

Donald Macrae – crofter, 'This is a hard working man and would do well in Canada: is honest, obliging and young.'

Widow Macrae – crofter, 'One I would willingly be rid of: is about 50 years of age.'

Donald McCaskill – no land, 'Still an active man but poor. This family are very promising, of good report and tolerably educated.'

Widow Chisholm – no land, 'A poor creature but not old; is honest and industrious.'

Widow Macdonald – no land, 'An old woman and a really good daughter.'

NOTE : the original list of tenants for Rhundunan and other farms is in the MacLeod Muniments.

SOAY TENANTS, 1887

Croft	Tenant	Cows	Rent
1.	Alexander Macrae	1	£1 10s
2.	Lachlan Macrae	1	£1 10s
3.	Angus Stewart	2	£2 10s
4.	John Stewart	1	£1 10s
5.	John Macrae	2	£2 10s
6.	Widow Macrae	2	£2 10s
7.	Ann Mackay	1	£1 10s
8.	Widow Mackay	2	£2 10s
9.	Ronald Macdonald	1	£1 10s
10.	John Macdonald	1	£1 10s
11.	Donald Maclean	1	£1 10s
12.	Widow Campbell	2	£2 10s
13.	Donald Macrae	2	no rent
14.	John Campbell	1	£1 10s
15.	John Campbell	2	£2 10s
16.	Donald Cameron	2	no rent
17.	Kate Macrae	1	£1 10s
18.	Alexander McCaskill	3	£3 10s
19.	Christina McRaw	1	£1 10s
		29	£33 10s

NOTE: Donald Macrae was excused rent for lodging the landlord's shepherd and Donald Cameron for his services as ferryman. There were, in addition, four other families staying at Soay at this date who paid no rent.

RENT ASSESSMENT, 1893

Crofter	Acres	Cows	Current Rent	Fair Rent
John Macrae	1	2	£2 10s	£2
John Campbell	1	2	£2 10s	£1 15s
Donald Macrae	1	2	£2 10s	£2
Donald Campbell	0.5	1	£1 10s	£1
John Macdonald	1	2	£2 10s	£2
Angus Stewart	1	2	£2 10s	£2
Neil Campbell	0.5	1	£1 10s	£1
Alexander McCaskill	1.5	3	£3 10s	£2 15s
Donald Cameron	1	2	£2 10s	£1 15s
Ronald Macdonald	0.5	1	£1 10s	£1
Ann Mackay	0.5	1	£1 10s	£1
John Stewart	1	2	£2 10s	£1 15s
	10.5	21	£27 0s	£20 0s

WHO THEY WERE

McCASKILL John – tacksman of Rhundunan, *s.* of John McCaskill and Janet Beaton: *m.* Catherine MacLeod of Drynoch: died 23 February 1775.

McCASKILL Kenneth – tacksman of Rhundunan, *s.* of the above: *m.* Christina MacLeod of Leasol: died 1 March 1841.

McCASKILL Donald – tacksman of Rhundunan, *s.* of the above: *m.* Colina McCaskill of Tallisker: died in New Zealand 24 February 1883.

McCASKILL Hugh – tacksman of Rhundunan, *s.* of Dr Donald McCaskill and Jane Campbell: brother-in-law of the above: *m.* Jessie Mackinnon of Corry: died 29 March 1863.

CAMERON Donald – tenant of Glenbrittle farm 1854–84: from Barcaldine, Argyllshire.

MACDONALD John – tenant of Glenbrittle farm 1906–21: from Duntulm in Skye.

WISHART Frederick – tenant of Glenbrittle farm 1921–29: from Elgin, Morayshire.

MACMILLAN Ewen – farm manager for Kenneth McCaskill: from Lochaber.

MACKINNON Charles – farm manager for Hugh McCaskill: from Strath in Skye.

LAIDLAW Henry – farm manager for MacLeod Estate: from Ross-shire.

McCASKILL Peter – sheep manager for Hugh McCaskill: *m.* Ann Macmillan of Camasunary: born in Brittle: lived at the Shepherd's Cot.

CAMERON Duncan – sheep manager for Donald Cameron: *m.* Jessie Macbean of Morven: born in Glenorchy: lived at the Shepherd's Cot.

MEIKLE William – shooting tenant 1911–17: from Edinburgh: rebuilt Mission House.

MACINNES Neil – grazing tenant 1929–34: from Strathaird: built Carri Cottage.

POWRIE Robert – fishing tenant 1935–51: from Perth: built Salmon Station.

CAMERON John – fisherman and tailor, *s.* of Donald Cameron (shepherd) and Christina Stewart: *m.* Christina *d.* of Donald Chisholm of Soay in 1834: died 1878 aged 71 years.

CAMERON Donald – ferryman, *s.* of the above: *m.* Joanna Cameron of Glenelg: tenant croft 14: built the Carn: died 1918 aged 76 years.

CAMERON Kenneth – postmaster, *s.* of the above: *m.* Marion Beaton: tenant croft 14: died 1941 aged 64 years: widow and sons evacuated to Mull.

CAMPBELL Neil – boatbuilder, *s.* of John Campbell (tailor) and Rachel Cameron: *m.* Janet Cameron of Soay in 1819: came to Soay from Husedale by L. Eynort: died 1865 aged 80 years.

CAMPBELL John – fiddler, *s.* of the above: *m.* Mary MacIntyre of Glenelg: lived at Burnside: died at Gairloch in 1888, aged 58 years, whilst playing the fiddle aboard the steamer *Fusilier*.

CAMPBELL Sandy – merchant seaman, *s.* of the above: *m.* Margaret Morrison: tenant croft 16: lived at Burnside: evacuated to Mull: died 1964 aged 80 years.

CAMPBELL Alexander – fisherman, *s.* of Neil Campbell and Christina McCaskill: *m.* Christina Mackinnon of Strath: born in Glen Drynoch: lived in the Old Village: died 1877 aged 67 years.

CAMPBELL Roderick – fisherman, *s.* of Donald Campbell (cottar) and Catherine MacLeod: *m.* Christina Macphie:

came to Soay from Carbost by L. Harport: lived in the Old Village: died 1873 aged 86 years.

CAMPBELL Donald – seaman, *s*. of the above: *m*. Mary Cameron of Carbost: killed in an accident at Greenock in 1879, aged 53 years.

CAMPBELL Donald – crofter fisherman, *s*. of the above: *m*. Jane MacInnes of Minginish: tenant croft 12: built Lagaphuirt: died 1940 aged 73 years.

CAMPBELL Alexander – crofter fisherman, *s*. of the above: unmarried: tenant croft 12: evacuated to Mull in 1953 but subsequently returned to Skye.

CHISHOLM Harry – fisherman, *s*. of Donald Chisholm (cottar) and Janet Mackay: unmarried: parents *m*. at Soay in 1802: lived near the Carn burn: died 1874 aged 67 years.

CHISHOLM Sandy – shepherd, *s*. of James Chisholm (shepherd) and Catherine Stewart: *m*. as his 2nd wife Jane Macdonald: born in Brittle: died 1871 aged 82 years.

MACLEAN Donald – fisherman, *s*. of Donald Maclean and Catherine Macrae: *m*. Mary Maclean: lived in the Old Village: died 1891 aged 85 years.

MORRISON Donald – labourer, *s*. of Angus Morrison and Margaret MacIntyre: *m*. Christina Chisholm: lived in the Old Village: died 1877 aged 72 years.

MORRISON Norman – fisherman, *s*. of Angus Morrison and Mary MacLeod: *m*. Marion Macdonald: lived in the Old Village: died 1879 aged 71 years.

McCASKILL Donald – fishcurer, *s*. of John McCaskill (soldier) and Euphemia Macpherson: *m*. Marion *d*. of Donald Macdonald of Soay in 1819: came to Soay from Borline by L. Eynort: died 1870 aged 84 years.

McCASKILL Sandy – crofter fisherman, *s*. of the above:

unmarried: tenant croft 18: built Ceann a Stigh: died 1913 aged 86 years.

McCASKILL Kenneth – ferryman, *s.* of Peter Macdonald (yachtmaster) and Christina McCaskill: nephew of the above: *m.* Christina Morrison: tenant croft 18: died 1939 aged 70 years.

McCASKILL John – crofter fisherman, *s.* of the above: *m.* Jemima, *d.* of Donald Campbell of Soay: tenant croft 18: evacuated to Mull: died 1977 aged 74 years.

MACDONALD Margaret – cottar, *d.* of Donald Macdonald and Christina McCaskill: *m.* Donald Macdonald: lived with a *d.* Christina near the Shepherd's Cot: died 1865 aged 90 years.

MACDONALD Neil – fisherman, *s.* of Donald Macdonald and Ann Gillies: *m.* as his 2nd wife Margaret MacLeod of Miodle: born at Soay: lived in the Old Village: died 1877 aged 85 years.

MACDONALD Donald – fisherman, *s.* of Ronald Macdonald (blacksmith) and Marion Macdonald: *m.* Margaret MacLeod: came to Soay from Trien by L. Harport: lived in the Old Village: died 1873 aged 66 years.

MACDONALD Ronald – fisherman, *s.* of the above: unmarried: tenant croft 9: built Rhu' Alasdair: died 1918 aged 76 years.

MACDONALD Donald – fisherman, *s.* of Ronald Macdonald and Euphemia Macdonald: nephew of the above: *m.* Annie MacIver: tenant croft 9: died 1950 aged 76 years: a *s.* Donald, evacuated to Mull.

MACDONALD Ronald – fisherman, *s.* of Ronald Macdonald (blacksmith) and Marion Macdonald: *m.* Effy *d.* of Roderick Campbell of Soay: came to Soay from Trien by L. Harport: lived in the Old Village: died 1863 aged 40 years.

MACDONALD John – crofter fisherman, *s.* of the above:

m. Christina *d.* of Donald Macrae of Soay: tenant croft 10: built Meadowbank: died 1942 aged 86 years.

MACDONALD Ronald – fisherman, *s.* of the above: unmarried: tenant croft 10: lived at Craignure after evacuation to Mull in 1953.

MACKAY John – cottar, *s.* of Christopher Mackay and Catherine MacLeod: *m.* Annie Cameron: lived in the Old Village: died 1858 aged 83 years.

MACKAY Christopher – fisherman, *s.* of the above: *m.* Hannah Mackinnon of Tobermory: lived in the Old Village: died 1877 aged 74 years.

MACKAY Ann – crofter, *d.* of the above : *m.* Malcolm Lamont at Cumbrae: tenant crofts 7&8: died 1924 aged 78 years.

MACRAE Rachel – crofter, d. of Finlay Chisholm and Marion Chisholm: *m.* Donald Macrae: came to Soay from Husedale by L. Eynort: lived at the Carri end: died 1870 aged 83 years.

MACRAE Lachlan – catechist, *s.* of the above: *m.* Flora Munro: born at Husedale by L. Eynort: lived at the Carri end: died 1893 aged 79 years.

MACRAE Alexander – shepherd, *s.* of Farquhar Macrae (farmer) and Marion Macrae: *m.* Jessie *d.* of Rachel Macrae of Soay: brother-in-law of the above: came to Soay from Camasunary: died 1902 aged 96 years.

MACRAE Donald – fisherman, *s.* of Neil Macrae (shepherd) and Effy Macrae: *m.* Janet *d.* of Donald Macdonald of Soay in 1832: came to Soay from Drynoch: lived at the Carri end: died 1879 aged 74 years.

MACRAE Donald – yachtsman, *s.* of the above: *m.* Christina *d.* of Alexander Campbell of Soay: tenant croft 13: built Leac Mhor: died 1911 aged 73 years.

MACRAE Neil – crofter fisherman, *s.* of the above: unmarried: tenant croft 13: evacuated to Mull: died 1961 aged 81 years.

STEWART John – seaman, *s.* of John Stewart (shepherd) and Mary Campbell: unmarried: lived with a sister near Shepherd's Cot: died 1874 aged 85 years.

STEWART Angus – fisherman, *s.* of Malcolm Stewart (joiner) and Ann Stewart: *m.* Jessie MacLeod: came to Soay from Sataran by L. Harport: lived at the Carri end: died 1882 aged 74 years.

STEWART John – fisherman, *s.* of the above: *m.* Euphemia Matheson: tenant croft 4 at the Carri end: died 1914 aged 80 years.

STEWART Rev. John – minister, *s.* of the above: *m.* Isobella MacLeod: *ed.* Soay school, High School and the University of Glasgow: served Tiree, Small Isles, Skye and in Canada: died 1933 aged 73 years.

NOTE : There was an island character, long remembered, called the Big Man of Soay. This was Kenneth McCaskill, son of Donald and Marion McCaskill, who was born in 1835. He is reputed to have weighed 40 stone and it is said that he was forever wearing the kilt since he could find no trousers to fit him.

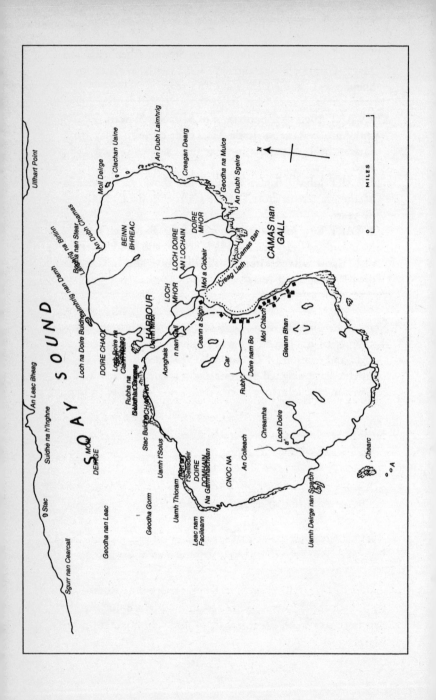

Ulfhart Point

SOAY SOUND

An Leac Bheag

Suidhe na h'Inghne

Sgurr nan Cearcall

Stac

SOAY BEAG

Geodha nan Leac

Geodha Gorm

Uamh Thioram

Leac nam Faoileann

Uamh r'Solus

DOIRE NA GAOITHE

Bare Sail Seoir

CNOC NA FAOILINN

An Coileach

Chreamha

Loch Doire a'

Uamh Deirge nan Sgarbh

Cheare

A

Gleann Bhan

Doire nam Bo

Mol Chladh

Car

Rubh'

Loch na Doire Buidhe

Laimhrig nan Damh

Geodha na Bifilinn

Geodha nan Stear

An Dubh Chamas

Moll Deirge

Clachan Uaine

An Dubh Laimhrig

Creagan Dearg

Geodha na Muice

An Dubh Sgeire

BEINN BHREAC

DOIRE MHOR

LOCH DOIRE AN LOCHAIN

LOCH MHOR

DOIRE CHAOL

Mol a Clobair

Creag Liath

Camas Ban

CAMAS nan GALL

Logh Doire na Clann Mhuig

Rubha na Clebamha

Stac Buidhe

DOIRE CHAIR

HARBOUR

Aonghais

n nan Gall

Ceann a' Sligh

N

MILES

0   1

LOCAL PLACE-NAMES

The island is to be found in the *Atlas Novus* of 1654 and Murdoch Mackenzie's *Maritime Survey* of 1776, but the first map of real value is Charles Stewart's *Plan of the Barony of Minginish*, drawn in 1810. Fifty years later Cmdr James Wood charted local waters for the Admiralty and this produced the first map of the island on the 6" scale. The Ordnance Survey did the land survey in the year 1877.

James Wood made a list of place-names for Soay with translation and remarks whereas the Ordnance surveyors compiled a *Name Book for the Parish of Bracadale*. The only published work on the subject is A.R. Forbes' *Place Names of Skye and Adjacent Islands*. This was produced in 1923. There are a great many names which do not appear on OS sheets or Admiralty charts. Some of them have been included here:

Acairseid Soa (Soay Harbour) – a narrow creek less than three hundred feet in breadth, frequented by heron. It has 12.6 acres of tidal water and there is a bar at the entrance. The Fish Store was built in 1849.

Allt Doire nam Bo (Stream of the Cattle Grove) – flows past the school and the largest stream on Soay.

Allt na Dubh Sgeir (the Burn of the Black Skerry) – issues into Strangers' Bay near the Skerry. A good spot for winklers.

Allt na Leac (Flagstone Stream) – spills as a waterfall into the Sound on the Skye side across from Soay Harbour. On the braes of this stream fires were lit to summon boats from the island.

Allt Sine (Jane's Burn) – the stream in Brittle in which Jane Chisholm of Soay was drowned en route for Leac in 1872.

An Coileach, A' Chearc (the Cock and Hen) – submerged rocks lying two cables south of the Stirks but visible at low water.

An Dubh Chamas (Black Harbour) – a small bight affording an anchorage within the Sound of Soay.

An Dubh Laimhrig (the Dark Landing Place) – on the island's north-east coast, frequented by otters and seals.

An Dubh Sgeire (the Black Skerry) – a roost for cormorants. In a cove just beyond this hazard the schooner *Woodman* was wrecked in the year 1868. Traces of her cargo of slates can still be found.

An Leac Bheag (the Small Flagstone) – a rocky protrusion on the Skye side of the Sound opposite Soay Harbour, used as a landing stage by ferrymen.

Bagh Clann Neill (MacNeil's Bay) – colonised by seals. The lone house belonged to a shepherd family who gave the place its name. The sheep fank was built about 1870.

Beinn Bhreac (the Speckled Mount) – 465 feet and Soay's highest hill with steep woods on the north face. There is a triangulation pillar at the top.

Bogha nan Gall (Strangers' Reef) – off the south-east coast and a favourite spot for beachcombers. The sea current passing between Eigg and Rhum splits on Soay in this area.

Bogha nan Stearnall (Seabirds' Reef) – at the south-east tip of the island near the head of the Dyke.

Cairidh (Fish Trap) – a stone weir at the southern end of the township used to catch herring, saithe and other fish in the old days. A 50 lb salmon was taken here once.

Camas Ban (the White Cove) – on the north side of the main bay and a good spot for driftwood.

Camas nan Gall (Bay of Strangers) – the main bay with stony beaches and white sand below the tides, frequented by oyster catchers, eider duck, and the hoodie crow.

Caolas Eilean (the Narrows of the Island) – the land between the Harbour and Loch Mhor, used in the old days to grow potatoes.

Carn (Cairn) – the old post office and home of the Cameron family who ran it.

Carn nan Gall (Height of Strangers) – a vantage point overlooking the main bay.

Carri – see *Cairidh*

Ceann a Stigh (House at the Head) – home of the McCaskills of Soay and site of a one time shop.

Ceann na h-Acairseid (Head of the Anchorage) – the neck of land between the Harbour and Strangers' Bay, just 380 yards across.

Clachan Uaine (the Green Stones) – giant boulders at the north-east corner, made of gabbro and deposited by a glacier.

Cnoc Ailean (Meadow Knoll) – on the north side of the island near the Grove of the Lochs.

Cnoc na h-Acairseid (Harbour Knoll) – a vantage point for viewing the Harbour.

Cnoc na Moil Deirge (Hill of the Red Bank) – named for the rock exposed on its flanks. The sandstone of Soay is far older than the Coolin hills and attains a thickness of over 3,000 feet.

Creag a' Chapuill (the Mare's Crag) – on the Skye side of the Sound near the Rhu. The cave below its summit was used by Stone Age knappers and Iron Age smelters.

Creagan Dearg (the Red Crag) – on the north-east coast between the Black Skerry and the Green Stones.

Creagan Dubh (the Black Crag) – in Soay Harbour near the waterfall on the west side.

Creag Liath (the Grey Cliff) – on the north side of the main bay between Shepherd's Beach and the White Cove.

Doire Chaol (the Narrow Thicket) – stone arrowheads have been found in the peat bogs here. *Creag Bhan* rises above it.

Doire Domhain (the Deep Thicket) – slopes down towards the Sound near Seagulls' Perch. *Cnocan Breac* rises above it to 307 feet.

Doire Mhor (the Great Thicket) – a woody dell formed by a fault running between the Black Skerry and Black Harbour.

Doire nam Bo (the Grove of the Cattle) – the glen through which the burn of that name passes. A habitat for the green hairstreak butterfly.

Geodha Choit (Boat Cove) – on the south east coast near the head of the Dyke.

Geodha Creagag (the Steep Rocky Chasm) – a deep rift on the coast opposite the South Stirk rocks.

Geodha Gorm (Green Creek) – an old quarry opposite the North Stirk rocks. In the farm lease of 1839 the landlord reserved the right to work Soay stone but accepted liability for damage caused to crops or livestock.

Geodha na h'Airigh (Cove of the Pasture) – on the Skye side of the Sound below the Garsbheinn, with large waterfall and rounded pebbles on the beach.

Geodha na Muice (the Sow's Creek) – on the north-east coast a short distance from the Black Skerry.

Geodha nan Leac (Flagstone Cove) – on the west coast south of Seagulls' Perch. Stone taken from the quarries in this sector went to Dunvegan Castle.

Gleann Bhan (the Fair Glen) – a well wooded dale running between Black Point Loch and the Old Village.

Lagaphuirt (Hollow Port) – home of the Campbells of Soay overlooking Strangers' Bay.

Laimhrig an Fhiona (the Boggy Landing Ground) – at the head of Soay Harbour on the west side.

Laimhrig na Birlinn (Landing Place for the Barge) – on the north coast to the west of the Black Harbour.

Laimhrig nan Damh (Landing Place for the Oxen) – cattle came ashore here after crossing from Brittle.

Leac Mhor (the Great Flagstone) – landing cove for the Old Village with bays for boats. The house of the name belonged to the Macraes.

Leac nam Faoileann (Seagulls' Perch) – at the north-west corner close to the former cod banks. The Sound is a mile and a half wide at this end.

Leac Stearnall (Lighting Place of Seabirds) – a rock shelf near the south-east corner of the island.

Lochan na Teanga Riabhaich (Loch of the Spotted Tongue) – shaped as named and spotted for the mass of water lilies on it.

Loch an Rubha Duibh (Black Point Loch) – a stream from the loch served the Old Village which otherwise depended on wells for its water supply.

Loch Doire na Sealbhag (Loch of the Sorrel Grove) – close to the cliff tops on the south coast. A habitat for scotch argus butterflies.

Loch Doire a' Chreamha (Loch of the Garlic Grove) – nearly 8 acres in extent and largest of the inland lochs. On the south side there is a mineral spring with curative properties. Garlic Grove lies to the north of the loch.

Loch Doire an Lochain (Loch of the Grove of the Loch) – stocked with trout but fished out by heron.

Loch Feith an Fhiona (Loch of the Morass) – a slough which drains into the Loch of the Garlic Grove.

Loch Mhor (the Great Loch) – near the Harbour. The islet at the centre was the site of a blacksmith's foundry. A stone causeway connected this to the shore on the east side of the loch.

Loch na Doire Buidhe (Loch of the Golden Grove) – frequented by moorhen and wild duck.

Loch na Doire Mhor (Loch of the Great Grove) – found in the grove of that name. Habitat for the small pearl-bordered fritillary.

Loch na h'Airde (Loch of the Point) – across the Sound at the Rhu. A canal connects the loch to the sea.

Loch na h'Uamha Crioma (Loch of the Round Shelter) – one winter's day a man fell through the ice on this loch and was drowned.

Moil Deirge (Red Stone Beach) – a raised beach with stones of that colour. A nesting ground for seabirds.

Mol a Ciobair (Shepherd's Beach) – where the ruin of the Shepherd's Cot is to be found in which visitors to Soay often stayed. A good spot for mussels.

Mol Chlach (the Stone Pile) – the raised beach directly in front of the Old Village, frequented by rabbits, otters, toads and shrews.

Mol Mhor (the Great Stone Beach) – across the Sound at the foot of the Garsbheinn.

Na Gamhnaichean (the Stirks) – prominent rocks off the south west coast. The highest is 6 feet above high water.

Port an Rubha (Port of the Point) – across the Sound at the Rhu directly below the Dun. The port is protected from the west by the Great Skerry.

Port an t'Seilisdeir (Port of the Water Flags) – near this port some circular ruins mark the last resting place of seamen washed ashore long ago. They are called *Tobtha an Duine*.

Rubh' Alasdair (Alexander's Point) – called after Alasdair Macrae who was drowned here as a boy. The house of the name was the last thatched dwelling to be occupied. It belonged to the Macdonalds.

Rubh' Aonghais (Angus' Point) – the most southerly point on the island but nobody now remembers who Angus was.

Rubha Dubh (Black Point) – the proper name for the Old Village which once housed nine families. In the 1930s the ruins were used to make a film about the clearances.

Rubha na h'Uamha Crioma (Point of the Round Shelter) – near the entrance to the Harbour, patrolled by ravens.

Sgurr nan Cearcall (the Cliff of Hoops) – on the Skye side of the Sound near the Rhu.

Slochd Dubh (the Black Pit) – over at the Rhu. A ditch formed by a fault running across the headland.

Soay Sound – three quarters of a mile at its narrowest point and about three miles in length. The sea current almost always takes a westerly course.

Stac (the Stack) – on the Skye side of the Sound. More of a stump than a pillar and made of basalt.

Stac Buidhe (the Yellow Stack) – in the Sound to the west of the Harbour entrance but east of the Deep Thicket.

Suidhe na h'Inghne (the Maiden's Seat) – across the Sound a short distance from the Flagstone.

Uamh Brian (Brian's Den) – on the south-east coast near the head of the Dyke. A low wall protects the inside from the elements but nobody now remembers who Brian was.

Uamh Criom (the Round Shelter) – in the Sound to the west of the Harbour near the point of that name.

Uamh Deirge nan Sgarbh (Red Cave of the Scarts) – on the west coast near the North Stirk rocks.

Uamh nan Gobhar (the Goats' Shelter) – a cliff overhang on the beach between Meadowbank and Burnside cottages. There were wild goats on Soay at one time.

Uamh Mhor (the Large Cave) – on the south coast to the east of Angus' Point.

Uamh Thioram (the Dry Cave) – in the Sound to the east of the Deep Thicket.

Uamh t'Solus (the Light Cave) – in the Sound a short distance from the Yellow Stack.

Ulfhart Point (Howling Point) – at the foot of the Garsbheinn and named for the noise of the wind at this corner.

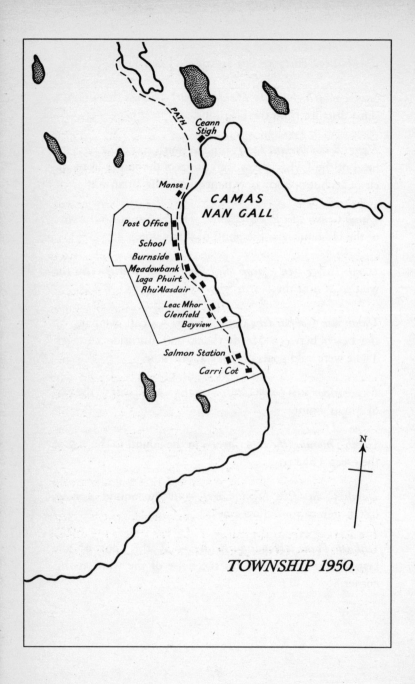

PATH

Ceann
Stigh

Manse

CAMAS
NAN GALL

Post Office

School
Burnside
Meadowbank
Laga Phuirt
Rhu'Alasdair

Leac Mhor
Glenfield
Bayview

Salmon Station

Carri Cot

N

TOWNSHIP 1950.

AN OLD DISPUTE

At the head of Loch Scavaig is the Hill of Strife (Sgurr na Stri), which takes its name from an old dispute between MacLeod of Dunvegan and the Mackinnons of Strath as to the true boundary of their respective clans. The Mackinnons claimed the Mad Burn (Allt Chaoich) near Coruisk as the march whereas the MacLeods claimed the glen between Camasunary and Sligachan.

Early in the eighteenth century the two chiefs met to settle things amicably and a line running north of a green knoll at Port of Shadows (Port Sgaile) was chosen. A young boy was then fetched from Soay and thrashed on the spot to keep the new march in remembrance. His name was Angus MacInnes and ever afterwards he was known in the district as MacIan Oig na Hain.

In 1876 a great granddaughter of Angus gave sworn testimony on the subject. She was Mary Macdonald who lived in Glenbrittle. In her early days she had lived at Soay and was frequently employed by McCaskill to collect his goats at Scavaig. When she was fourteen years old she went to Scavaig from Soay to cut seaware to make kelp, and the spot was pointed out to her.

The Port Sgaile boundary was laid down clearly in the farm lease for 1792 but Kenneth McCaskill, in the interest of good neighbourliness and to save trouble, generally kept the Scavaig river as the march. Today the river is the official boundary between the parish of Bracadale and the parish of Strath.